The villas of the ancients illustrated. By Robert Castell.

Robert. Castell

ECCO

PRINT EDITIONS

Gale ECCO Print Editions

Relive history with *Eighteenth Century Collections Online*, now available in print for the independent historian and collector. This series includes the most significant English-language and foreign-language works printed in Great Britain during the eighteenth century, and is organized in seven different subject areas including literature and language; medicine, science, and technology; and religion and philosophy. The collection also includes thousands of important works from the Americas.

The eighteenth century has been called "The Age of Enlightenment." It was a period of rapid advance in print culture and publishing, in world exploration, and in the rapid growth of science and technology – all of which had a profound impact on the political and cultural landscape. At the end of the century the American Revolution, French Revolution and Industrial Revolution, perhaps three of the most significant events in modern history, set in motion developments that eventually dominated world political, economic, and social life.

In a groundbreaking effort, Gale initiated a revolution of its own: digitization of epic proportions to preserve these invaluable works in the largest online archive of its kind. Contributions from major world libraries constitute over 175,000 original printed works. Scanned images of the actual pages, rather than transcriptions, recreate the works *as they first appeared.*

Now for the first time, these high-quality digital scans of original works are available via print-on-demand, making them readily accessible to libraries, students, independent scholars, and readers of all ages.

For our initial release we have created seven robust collections to form one the world's most comprehensive catalogs of 18th century works.

Initial Gale ECCO Print Editions collections include:

History and Geography
Rich in titles on English life and social history, this collection spans the world as it was known to eighteenth-century historians and explorers. Titles include a wealth of travel accounts and diaries, histories of nations from throughout the world, and maps and charts of a world that was still being discovered. Students of the War of American Independence will find fascinating accounts from the British side of conflict.

Social Science

Delve into what it was like to live during the eighteenth century by reading the first-hand accounts of everyday people, including city dwellers and farmers, businessmen and bankers, artisans and merchants, artists and their patrons, politicians and their constituents. Original texts make the American, French, and Industrial revolutions vividly contemporary.

Medicine, Science and Technology

Medical theory and practice of the 1700s developed rapidly, as is evidenced by the extensive collection, which includes descriptions of diseases, their conditions, and treatments. Books on science and technology, agriculture, military technology, natural philosophy, even cookbooks, are all contained here.

Literature and Language

Western literary study flows out of eighteenth-century works by Alexander Pope, Daniel Defoe, Henry Fielding, Frances Burney, Denis Diderot, Johann Gottfried Herder, Johann Wolfgang von Goethe, and others. Experience the birth of the modern novel, or compare the development of language using dictionaries and grammar discourses.

Religion and Philosophy

The Age of Enlightenment profoundly enriched religious and philosophical understanding and continues to influence present-day thinking. Works collected here include masterpieces by David Hume, Immanuel Kant, and Jean-Jacques Rousseau, as well as religious sermons and moral debates on the issues of the day, such as the slave trade. The Age of Reason saw conflict between Protestantism and Catholicism transformed into one between faith and logic -- a debate that continues in the twenty-first century.

Law and Reference

This collection reveals the history of English common law and Empire law in a vastly changing world of British expansion. Dominating the legal field is the *Commentaries of the Law of England* by Sir William Blackstone, which first appeared in 1765. Reference works such as almanacs and catalogues continue to educate us by revealing the day-to-day workings of society.

Fine Arts

The eighteenth-century fascination with Greek and Roman antiquity followed the systematic excavation of the ruins at Pompeii and Herculaneum in southern Italy; and after 1750 a neoclassical style dominated all artistic fields. The titles here trace developments in mostly English-language works on painting, sculpture, architecture, music, theater, and other disciplines. Instructional works on musical instruments, catalogs of art objects, comic operas, and more are also included.

The BiblioLife Network

This project was made possible in part by the BiblioLife Network (BLN), a project aimed at addressing some of the huge challenges facing book preservationists around the world. The BLN includes libraries, library networks, archives, subject matter experts, online communities and library service providers. We believe every book ever published should be available as a high-quality print reproduction; printed on-demand anywhere in the world. This insures the ongoing accessibility of the content and helps generate sustainable revenue for the libraries and organizations that work to preserve these important materials.

The following book is in the "public domain" and represents an authentic reproduction of the text as printed by the original publisher. While we have attempted to accurately maintain the integrity of the original work, there are sometimes problems with the original work or the micro-film from which the books were digitized. This can result in minor errors in reproduction. Possible imperfections include missing and blurred pages, poor pictures, markings and other reproduction issues beyond our control. Because this work is culturally important, we have made it available as part of our commitment to protecting, preserving, and promoting the world's literature.

GUIDE TO FOLD-OUTS MAPS and OVERSIZED IMAGES

The book you are reading was digitized from microfilm captured over the past thirty to forty years. Years after the creation of the original microfilm, the book was converted to digital files and made available in an online database.

In an online database, page images do not need to conform to the size restrictions found in a printed book. When converting these images back into a printed bound book, the page sizes are standardized in ways that maintain the detail of the original. For large images, such as fold-out maps, the original page image is split into two or more pages

Guidelines used to determine how to split the page image follows:

• Some images are split vertically; large images require vertical and horizontal splits.
• For horizontal splits, the content is split left to right.
• For vertical splits, the content is split from top to bottom.
• For both vertical and horizontal splits, the image is processed from top left to bottom right.

VILLAS

OF THE

ANCIENTS

ILLUSTRATED.

BY
R O B E R T C A S T E L L.

Vos sapere & solos aio bene vivere, quorum
Conspicitur nitidis fundata pecunia Villis.

Hor.

LONDON
Printed for the A U T H O R.
MDCCXXVIII.

TO THE

RIGHT HONOURABLE

RICHARD

EARL of *BURLINGTON.*

My LORD,

WHEN I confider Your great and univerfal Knowledge in the *Belles Arts,* it is not without a juft Apprehenfion of my own Defects, that I fubmit this fmall Performance to your Judgment; but when I again reflect that many Works of *Inigo Jones* and *Palladio's* had perifh'd but for Your Love to Architecture, I lay afide my Fears, and the rather as this Work is wholly founded on the Rules of the Ancients, for whom Your Lordfhip has on all Occafions manifefted the greateft Regard

The Authors who furnifh out the Materials for what I here prefent You, were, like Your Lordfhip, great Admirers of Arts, and for the fame Reafon too, becaufe they had Skill enough to difcern their Excellencies.

I

DEDICATION.

I shall think myself Happy, if while I am assisted with the Pieces of *Varro* and *Pliny*, (two Persons of eminent Rank in the *Roman* State) I may be thought worthy the Patronage of my Lord BURLINGTON, who is of no less Eminence in our Own; and I am confident there is no One so zealously devoted to these Ancients but will permit me to say, You excel them in this, They cultivated Arts while they yet flourish'd in their Glory, but You give them new Life when they languish, and even rescue them from Decay and Oblivion   I am,

My LORD,

Your Lordships most obedient

and most humble Servant,

ROBERT CASTELL.

THE
PREFACE.

A Defire I have long entertain'd of tranflating and explaining Vitruvius, determin'd me firft to fet about fome inferior Performance in
Architecture, as a neceffary Preparation to my entring on a Work
of fo much Labour and Difficulty And as I thought nothing could be more
proper for my Choice than fuch a Branch of the Art as that great Mafter
had been leaft Curious to explain, I refolved to take for my Subject the Rules
that were obferved in the fituating and difpofing of the Roman Villas, which
he fpeaks of only in a curfory Way, lib 6 cap 10. and to this End I have
been at the Pains to perufe many ancient Authors, who have treated more at
large of that Part, not the meaneft of the Architect's Bufinefs

Moft of the Roman Writers upon Agriculture that are remaining, have
thought fit, at the Beginning of their Works, to tell us what were to be confider'd in the Situation and Difpofition of Villas Cato, the eldeft of them
left the feweft Rules on that Head, and of the leaft Confeque ce, but Varro
that was the next after him, has been more ample and judicious in his obfervations, and feems to have laid the Foundation for what Columella, Palladius, and thofe feveral Greek Authors mention'd by Conftantine, have
fince wrote on that Subject He has difcours'd more fully than any of them
on thofe Parts of the Villa that were defign'd as well for the Pleafures of a
retir'd Life as the Conveniencies and Profits of Agriculture

Pliny the Younger alone has exceeded Varro in this Particular, he has
left us two Epiftles, containing an exact Defcription of his Villas of Laurentinum and Tufcum, and tho' we find not in him any direct Rules for the
Difpofition of the Villa Urbana or Country Houfe of Pleafure, yet he gives
us to underftand, that thofe Buildings were contriv'd according to the

b   ftricteft

The PREFACE.

strictest Rules of Art, and points out what were principally regarded in the placing and ordering of them, and how they were at once accommodated by the Architect for enjoying the Benefits, and for avoiding the Inconveniencies of the several Seasons. He speaks only of the Situation and Disposition of those Buildings, knowing his Friends to whom he wrote, could not but be sensible that the Rules laid down by Vitruvius with respect to Beauty and Proportion were equally to take Place in the City and Country.

I thought it proper to quote my Authorities at large, and especially the two Epistles of Pliny, which the Reader hath here both in Latin and English. And as I attempt only to shew the Distribution and Disposition of such Buildings, I have omitted to draw any Elevations and Sections but what are taken from the express Words of the Ancients, or are evidently necessary to illustrate the Meaning of some difficult Passages.

The whole work consists of three Parts. The first contains the Description of a Villa Urbana, or Country House of Retirement near the City, that was supplied with most of the Necessaries of Life from a neighbouring Market-Town. The second sets forth the Rules that were necessary to be observed by an Architect, who had the Liberty to chuse a Situation, and to make a proper Distribution of all Things in and about the Villa, but particularly with relation to the Farm House, which in this Sort of Buildings, according to the more ancient Roman Manner, was always join'd to the Master's House, or but very little remov'd from it. In the third Part is shewn the Description of another Villa Urbana, on a Situation very different from the former, with the Farm House and its Appurtenances so far remov'd as to be no Annoyance to it, and at the same Time so near as to furnish it conveniently with all Necessaries.

A

A

LIST

OF THE

SUBSCRIBERS.

A

EARL of Aylesford.

Earl of Arran

Honourable Richard Arundel, *Esq,*

John Aiflabie, *Esq, two Books*

Abel Alleyne, *Esq, five Books*

Thomas Afhby, *Esq,*

S; John St Aubyn, *Bart*

B

Lord Bruce

Lord Baltimore

Thomas Batfon, *Esq,*

John Baynes, *Esq, Serjeant at Law.*

Benjamin Benfon, *Esq,*

Edward Bram, *Esq,*

Martin Bladen, *Esq,*

Thomas Bladen, *Esq,*

Rowland Blackman, *Esq,*

Mr Thomas Bofwell

John Brampton, *Esq,*

John Bridges, *Esq,*

Peter Burrel, *Esq,*

C

Earl of Cardigan

Lord James Cavendifh

Honourable Sir Robert Clifton, *Knight of the* Bath

Honourable William Cecil, *Esq,*

Corpus Chrifti *College,* Oxford.

Sir Nicholas Carew, *Bart*

Mr Richard Chappel

John Clark, *Esq,*

Edward Cook, *Esq.*

D.

Dutchefs of Dorfet.

Earl of Derby

George Ducket, *Esq,*

E.

Earl of Effex

Mr Peter Ellam.

Mr John Ellam

F

Sir Piercy Freke, *Bart*

Honourable John Finch, *Esq, two Books.*

Honourable Mrs Finch.

Colonel Folliot

Stephen Fox, *Esq,*

George Fox, *Esq,*

Mr Paul Fourdrinier

Philip Frowde, *Esq;*

Mr Charles Frowde

G

Lady Betty Germain

Honourable Thomas Levefon Gower, *Esq;*

Honourable Baptift Levefon Gower, *Esq,*

Roger Gale, *Esq,*

John Gibbons, *Esq;*

Jofeph Gibbs, *Esq;*

Mr Philip Gilbert.

John Green, *Esq,*

Francis Gwyn, *Esq,*

Reverend Mr. Auguftine Gwyn.

H.

Sir Nevil Hickman, *Bart*

John

A LIST *of the* SUBSCRIBERS.

Honourable Ferdinand Haftings, *Efq*,
Honourable Robert Herbert, *Efq*,
Henry Harrington, *Efq, two Books.*
Thomas Hafket, *Efq*,
Richard Heath, *Efq, two Books*
Mr. Thomas Heath
        Hefketh, *Efq*;
Mr Thomas Howard
Mr William Howfon

J

St John's *College*, Cambridge
Michael Jackfon, *Efq*,
Charles Jennens, *Efq*,
        Joye, *Efq*,

K.

Lord Kinfale
Mr Sidney Kennon
Richard Knight, *Efq*,

L

Lord Limerick
John Law, *Efq*,
Richard Lely, *Efq*,
Mr John Lely
David Lewis, *Efq*,
Charles Lockear, *Efq*,

M.

Duke of Montagu
Lord Middleton
Lord William Mannors
Sir Chriftopher Mufgrave, *Bart. two Books.*
Honourable Buffey Manfel, *Efq*,
Captain Martin
Littleton Pointz Meynel, *Efq*,
Mr John Mead
Thomas More, *Efq*,
William Mofes, *Efq, two Books.*

N.

Duke of Norfolk
Sir Clobery Noel, *Bart*
Mr. Richard Nicholfon.

O

Earl of Oxford
James Oglethorpe, *Efq, two Books*

P

Earl of Pembroke
Honourable Colonel Paget
Sir Herbert Packington, *Bart*
Robert Packer, *Efq*,
Winchcomb Howard Packer, *Efq*,
Erafmus Philips, *Efq*,

R

Langham Rokeby, *Efq*,
Mr Henry Ricard

S

Duke of Somerfet, *fix Books*
Honourable Sir William Stanhope, *Knight of the* Bath
Honourable Sir Robert Sutton, *Knight of the* Bath
Sir Charles Sedley, *Bart*
Sir Edward Smyth, *Bart*
Matthew Snow, *Efq*,
George Stanley, *Efq*,

T.

       Thomas, *Efq*,
William Tryon, *Efq*,
Cholmly Turner, *Efq*,

V.

Honourable Henry Vane, *Efq*,
John Vanderbank, *Efq*,

W.

Abel Walter, *Efq*,
Mr Peter Waldo.
John Wefton, *Efq*,
Henry Wefton, *Efq*,

Y

Reverend Mr. Richard Younger

T H E

THE

VILLAS of the ANCIENTS

ILLUSTRATED.

PART I.

LIBER II EP. XVII.	BOOK II EP. XVII.
C Plinius Gallo suo, S.	**Pliny** *to* Gallus, *Health.*

MIRARIS cur me Laurentinum, vel (fi ita mavis) Laurens meum tantopere delectet· defines mirari, cum cognoveris Gratiam ' Villæ, Opportunitatem Loci, Litoris Spatium,

YOU wonder I am so much delighted with Laurentinum, or, if you had rather, Laurens, *my Country-Seat But you will cease to do so, when you are acquainted with the Beauty of the* ' Villa, *the*

' *Villa.*] *Varro, lib 1 cap 3* tells us from whence this Word is deriv'd His Words are these *Villa, quod in eam convehuntur fructus, & evehuntur, cum veneunt A quo rustici etiam*

nunc

tium Decem & septem milli
bus Passuum ab Urbe secedit, ut,
peractis quae agenda fuerint, salvo
jam & composito die possis ibi manere. Aditur non una via, nam
& Laurentina & Ostiensis eadem
ferunt, sed Laurentina a quarto
decimo Lapide, Ostiensis ab undecimo relinquenda est. Utrimque excipit Iter aliqua ex parte
arenosum, Jumentis paulo gravius & longius, Equo breve &
molle. Varia hinc atque inde
facies, nam modo occurrentibus Sylvis Via coarctatur, modo
latissimis Pratis diffunditur & patescit. multi Greges Ovium, multi ibi Equorum Boumque Armenta,

the Conveniency of the Place, and the
Spaciousness of the Coast. It lies seventeen Miles from Rome, so that,
having finished the Business of the City, one may reach it with Ease and
Safety by the Close of the Day. There
are two Ways to it, for both the
Laurentine and the Ostian Road
will carry you thither. The first must
be left at the end of the tenth Mile,
and the latter at the thirteenth.
Whichever Road you take is partly sandy, something heavy and tedious for Carriages, but short and
easy to those that ride. The Country
on both Sides affords a great Variety of Views, in some Places the
Prospect is confin'd by Woods, in
others is extended over large and
spacious Meadows, where many
Flocks

... whereof it had its appellation, proper ... & Illam and Villam, quo Vehunt & unde
... A Villa according to ... Villa consisted of three Parts, viz. Urbana, Rustica &
Fructuaria. The first of which was that Part of the House, set apart for the Master's Use, the
second was for the Cattle and Servants that till'd the Land, and were employ'd in the more ordinary Services of the House, and the last consisted only of Repositories for Corn, Wine, Oyl, &c.
So ... the Villa Urbana, or House of Pleasure, was only a Country House of Pleasure,
built without any regard to the Villa Rustica, or any thing relating to Agriculture or Pasturage,
and though such Houses, according to the Opinion of Varro, lib. 3 cap. 1 did not deserve the
Name of Villa, yet it appears that in Pliny's Time they bore that Appellation. But Palladius
who lived ... author never uses that Word but when he speaks of that Part of the House
peculiarly called Pretorium Villae makes use of the Word Pretorium, to express the whole Villa,
which ... call Pretorium-Urbanum, by which he means only a House built in the Country,
with all the Members and Ornaments of those of the City.

A quarto decimo Lapide.] The Miles on the Roman Roads were distinguish'd by a Pillar, or
Stone set up at the End of each of them, which was mark'd with one or more Figures, signifying how far it was from the Millarium Aureum, a Pillar in the Forum near the Temple of Saturn,
which had on it the Figure I, so that the next Pillar to it, which was mark'd II was but one
Mile from the Standard Pillar, and consequently the XIV and XI Stones were but thirteen and
ten Miles from the Forum.

menta, quæ, Montibus Hyeme depulfa, Herbis & Tepore verno nitefcunt Villa ufibus capax, non fumptuofa Tutela: cujus in prima Parte 3 Atrium frugi, nec tamen fordidum; deinde 4 Porticus in 5 O Literæ Similitudinem circumactæ, quibus parvula fed feftiva 6 Area includitur. Egregium hæ adverfùm Tempeftates Receptaculum;

Flocks of Sheep and Herds of Cattle, that were driven from the Mountains by the Severity of the Weather, grow sleek and fat by the returning Warmth of the Spring, and the Richness of the Pasturage My Villa is large enough to afford a convenient, tho not sumptuous, Reception for my Friends The first thing that offers it self is a plain, tho' not mean 3 Atrium, from thence you enter a 4 Porticus in form like the Letter 5 O, which surrounds a small but pleasant 6 Area. This is an excellent Retreat

3 *Atrium*] By what *Vitruvius* says, *l* 6 *c* 10 it plainly appears that the *Atrium* was the firft Room of the Houfe, and lay juft beyond the *Veftibulum*, and, by the Rules he has given us for them, *c* 17 it is manifeft that tho' they were fometimes of different Proportions, they had one thing common to them all, which was, that a great Part of them was open at top In the Country, where they were not ftraitned for Room, the *Atrium* was what we call the *Fore-Court*, as this of *Pliny*'s appears to have been, and the *Atrium* was to be pafs'd before one could come to the *Veftibulum* It is not improbable but fome of thefe Fore-Courts had *Porticus* round them, like the *Ala* of the City *Atrium*, and were for Clients and thofe Servants to wait in, that were from thence call'd *Atrienfes* In *Rome* there were feveral Buildings that were call'd *Atria*, as the *Atrium Publicum*, *Atria Libertatis*, *Veftæ*, *Minervæ*, &c which very probably were fo call'd for the Refemblance they bore to thofe *Vitruvius* defcribes, or were Courts before Temples, or other Publick Buildings, furrounded by *Porticus*

4 *Porticus*] This was a common Name to all Buildings that had Walks under the Covert of a Roof or Cieling, fupported by Pillars or Pilafters, tho' differently call'd, according to the Difpofition of the Pillars When plac'd on the Outfide of a Building, as round fome of their Temples, it was call'd *Peripterium*, when thefe Ranges of Pillars were within a Room, as they were fometimes in their *Triclinia*, *Bafilicæ*, *Atria*, and Temples, the void Space betwixt the Pillars and the fide Walls was called *Ala* But when Pillars furrounded Courts, and had Walks betwixt them and the Walls, thefe Ranges of Pillars were called *Periftylia*, and the Walk betwixt was call'd a *Porticus*.

5 *O*] It appears by antient Infcriptions, that the *Romans* did not make this Letter exactly circular, but rather elliptical, the Form of which he therefore chofe, as moft eafily defcribing that of his *Porticus* For tho' *Ellipfis* is become a common Word, and is underftood by moft to fignify an oval Form, yet it truly fignifies no more than a Defect, as an Oval was a defective Circle, and wou'd have requir'd more Words for its Explanation, than *Pliny* thought fit to employ.

6 *Area*] This Word is deriv'd from *arendo*, and originally fignify'd a plain even Space laid out near the Farm-Houfe to dry the Corn in the Sun, for the making of which thofe *Roman* Authors that have wrote on Agriculture have given Directions. It was afterwards ufed for any Pavement *fub dio*, and furrounded by Buildings

culum; nam 7 Specularibus, ac multo magis imminentibus Tectis muniuntur. Est contra medius 8 Cavædium hilare; mox 9 Triclinium satis pulchrum, quod in Litus excurrit; ac si quando 10 Africo Mare impulsum est, fractis jam & novissimis Fluctibus leviter adluitur:

Retreat in bad Weather; being shelter'd by 7 glaz'd Windows, but much more so by the Projection of the Roof. Against the middle of the Porticus *is a pleasant* 8 Cavædium; *beyond which is an handsome* 9 Triclinium, *that advances out upon the Shore; so that when the Sea is driven in by the Wind* 10 Africus, *its Foundation is*

Specularibus] The Commentators on this Epistle, who have taken notice of this Word, agree that it signifies a Window made of transparent Stone, as perhaps imagining that Glass was not then put to that Use; but if so, *Palladius* certainly would not have given Directions to his Husbandman to run the *Specularia* in the *Olearium*. For tho' there might probably have been more Plenty of those Stones among the Ancients than at present, yet it appears by *Pliny* the Naturalist's describing a Temple built with it as the greatest Rarity of his Time, and by the mention *Plutarch* makes of a Room in *Domitian*'s Palace which was lin'd with it, that it was not common enough for Husbandmen to purchase, so that it may be rather conjectur'd that *Specularia* signified nothing but Glass Windows that wanted no Shutters to keep out the Weather, and could always be seen through, as *Fenestræ* signify'd those where the Weather was kept out only by Shutters. *Columella* mentions raising Cucumbers with *Specularia*, and *Martial* takes notice that the *Romans* shelter'd their Rose Trees by them, as we at this Day make Green-houses to preserve our most valuable tender Trees.

Cavædium] To most of the *Roman* Villa's belong'd three sorts of Courts, viz. that before the House, which was call'd the *Atrium*, the Office-Court, or Farm-Yard, call'd *Chors*, and the Court within the House, call'd *Cavædium*, or *Cava Ædium*, being an Area surrounded by the Buildings of the House. The Similitude there was between the City *Atrium* and the *Cavædium*, being both open at top, has occasion'd several to imagine these Terms signify'd the same thing. But they may be satisfy'd to the contrary, if they will consult *Vitruvius*, lib. 6. where he tells us how many sorts of *Cavædia* there were, and gives Directions for the City *Atrium*. The *Grecians*, who, by *Vitruvius*'s Account, had no *Atrium* in their Houses, were not without the *Cavædium*, which they call'd *Αυλη*, as being a Place *sub dio*. These Courts are by *Vitruvius*, in his Description of the *Grecian* Houses, lib. 6. cap. 10. call'd *Peristylia*, because surrounded by Pillars, but afterwards in the same Cap. speaking of the Passages that were betwixt the *Peristylia* and *Hospitalia*, where they entertain'd Strangers, he calls them *Mesaulæ, quod inter duas Aulas media sint interposita.*

9 *Triclinium*] This Room was originally so call'd from the three Beds it could contain, yet this Name was sometimes given to larger Eating Rooms, tho' they are by *Vitruvius* term'd *Œci* from οικος *Domus*, call'd so either from their extraordinary Size, or as they were commonly separated from the main Building, or only join'd to it by one Wall, might seem to be Houses themselves. Of these *Œci* there were three sorts in use among the *Romans*, viz. the *tetrastyle*, the *Corinthian*, and the *Egyptian*, of all which, and wherein they differ'd, *Vitruvius* gives an Account, l. 6. c. 5. Besides these common to the *Romans*, there was one sort that, in *Vitruvius*'s time, was only in use among the *Grecians*, viz. the *Cyzicen*, spoke of by him l. 6. c. 6. The Office of the *Triclinium* and *Œcos* was the same, viz. for Intertainments, yet it appears by *Vitr.* l. 6. c. 10. that the *Grecian* Ladies frequently pass'd the Hours allotted to their Needle Work in the *Œci*.

10 *Africus*] There being a Necessity for placing the *Roman* Winds round the following Plans, to them the Reader is referr'd, where may be seen how they agree with our Compass.

adluitur . undique Valvas, aut Fe-
neſtias non minores Valvis habet:
atque ita à Lateribus, à Fronte,
quaſi tria Maria proſpectat. A
tergo Cavædium, Porticum, Aream; Porticum ruiſus, mox Atrium, Sylvas, & longinquos reſpicit
Montes Hujus à lævi retractius
paulo, [11] Cubiculum eſt amplum:
deinde aliud minus, quod altera
Feneſtra admittit Orientem, Oc-
cidentem altera retinet: hæc &
ſubjacens Maie longius quidem,
ſed ſecurius intuetui Hujus Cubiculi, & Triclinii illius Objectu
includitur Angulus, qui puriſ-
ſimum Solem continet, & accen-
dit Hoc [12] Hybernaculum, hoc
etiam

is gently waſh'd by the laſt, ſpent and
broken Waves On every ſide are
Folding-Doors, or Windows as large
So that from the Front, and both
Sides, you have the View as it were
of three ſeveral Seas, and back-
wards is ſeen the Cavædium, the
Porticus, the Area; again the
Porticus, then the Atrium, and
laſtly, the Woods and diſtant
Mountains At the left hand of
the Triclinium, not ſo far advanced
towards the Sea, is a large [11] Cubiculum; beyond that a leſs, which
has one Window to the Riſing, and
another to the Setting Sun From
hence the Sea is ſeen at ſomething a
greater Diſtance, but with more Se-
curity from its Inclemencies The
Angle that this Cubiculum and Triclinium make by their Jettings out,
does not only retain, but add force
to, the warmeſt Rays of the Sun Here
is my [12] Hybernaculum, and the

B   Gym-

---

[11] *Cubiculum*] This Word in its general Acceptation is taken to ſignify nothing but a Bed chamber,
but is us'd by *Vitruvius*, and other Authors, as a common Name to all Rooms that were not for ſome
particular Office, ſuch is the *Triclinium*, *Atrium*, &c ſo that here it ſeems to have meant no more than
what at preſent is called a Room, and when a Bed-chamber was intended it was moſt often diſtinguiſh'd
as ſuch, as appears by *Pliny* in this Epiſtle, where he ſays, *Cubiculum noctis & ſomni*, and in the Deſcription of his *Tuſcan Villa* he calls one Room *Dormitorium Cubiculum*

[12] *Hybernaculum*] This Word is uſed by *Vitruvius*, to ſignify that Part of the Houſe which
by its Diſpoſition, was moſt proper to be inhabited during the Winter, as the other Appartments that
were turn'd to the *Eaſt* and *North*, were for the Summer, but here the Word ſignifies a Place out of
the Houſe made warm in Winter by the Sun

etiam [13] Gymnasium meorum est; ibi omnes silent Venti, exceptis qui Nubilum inducunt, & serenum antequam Usum Loci eripiunt Adnectitur Angulo Cubiculum in [14] Apsida curvatum, quod Ambitum Solis Fenestris omnibus sequitur Parieti ejus in Bibliothecæ speciem Armarium insertum est, quod non legendos Libros, sed	[13] Gymnasium *of my Family; which is never incommoded by any Winds, but those which bring in cloudy Weather, and destroy the, at other times, serene Situation of the Place Joining to this Angle is a* Cubiculum, *that jets out in an* [14] *Elliptick Form, from which gradually at all its Windows it receives the whole Course of the Sun It has in its Walls Repositories after the manner of Libraries,*

---

[13] *Gymnasium*] *Pausanias* informs us, that the *Grecians* had Places set apart in every City for public Exercise, which are by him call'd *Gymnasia*, from their exercising naked in them By *Vitruvius*, who gave the exact Description of one of these Places, they are call'd *Palæstra*, from the Exercise of the Ball that was used there In these Buildings they not only used bodily Exercise, but held Disputations in all Parts of polite Learning, and in them there were allotted Parts to the Philosophers and Poets, as well as to the Wrestlers The *Roman Thermæ* were but Imitations of these *Grecian Palæstra*, and consisted of as many and the same Parts, and, like the other, were design'd for public Exercise By this Passage of *Pliny* it appears, that these public Exercises were also used in their private Houses, and that the Place it self was call'd by the same Name the *Grecians* (from whom they borrow'd this Custom) gave to their Places of Exercise

[14] *Apsida*] This Word, which is often made use of by *Pliny* the Naturalist, *l 2* is an Astronomical Term, and is at present taken for those two Points in the Orbit of a Planet, one of which is farthest from, and the other nearest to the Sun For instance The Elliptick Orbit of the Earth being represented by the Figure *A B P D*, in one of whose Locus's, *O*, is plac'd the Sun, the Points *A, P*, are the Apsides, or those two Points in the Orbit of the Earth, one of which, *A*, is the farthest from, and the other, *P*, nearest to the Sun, *O* This is the strict Meaning of the Word, as used at present, but here it seems to signify the Round the Earth took, according to the *Ptolemaick* System, about this Planet

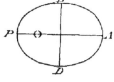

It is remarkable that, in the Description of the *Portico's* of this *Isle*, and in this Room where *Pliny* had occasion to mention a Form which we vulgarly call an Oval, and the Mathematicians an Ellipsis, from its being a defective Circle and one of the Conick Sections he is oblig'd to take the Method he has done to explain himself, by comparing the former to the Letter O, and this to that imaginary Curve in Astronomy, before-mention'd For though Ellipsis and Oval are become at present synonimous Terms to express this Curve, the former truly signifies in it self no more than a Defect, and the latter, strictly taken, means a Form in all respects equal to that of an Egg, and not the Periphery, and it was only the want of a Word to express this Form, that made *Vitruvius, l 6 c 5* in his Directions for the Ceiling of the *Corinthian Œcus* to say, *Circuli rotundi ad Ovatum & lumbata*.

fed lectitandos capit Adhæret
15 Dormitorium Membrum, Tranfitu interjacente, qui 16 fuspensus
& tabulatus, conceptum Vaporem
falubri Temperamento huc illuc
digerit & miniftrat. Reliqua Pars
Lateris hujus Servorum Liberto-
rumque ufibus detinetur, plerifs-
que tam mundis, ut accipere Hof-
pites poffint. Ex alio latere Cubiculum eft politiffimum: deinde
vel Cubiculum grande, vel modica 17 Cœnatio, quæ plurimo Sole, plurimo Mari lucet. Poft hanc
Cubiculum cum 18 Procœtone, Altitudine æftivum, Munimentis hybernum,

ries, containing Books, rather for A-
musement, than Study. Close to this
lies 15 the Dormitorium, with only a
void Space betwixt, which being
16 boarded and shelving, in a whol-
some manner tempers the concei-
ved Heat, and administers it to all
Parts of the Room The rest of this
side of the House is allotted to my
Freemen and Slaves, yet is for the
most part decent enough to receive my
Friends On the right-hand of the
Triclinium is a most elegant Cubiculum; and another either very large
Cubiculum, or moderate 17 Cœnatio;
which is much enlightened both by
the Sun and Sea After this is a Cubiculum with a 18 Procœton; 'tis
for

---

15 *Dormitorium Membrum*] This Room, when diftinguifh'd from the *Cubiculum*, was a Place fet apart for no other ufe than that of a Bed-chamber, which was not always imply'd in the Word *Cubiculum*, as has been before taken notice of.

16 *Suspensus & tabulatus*] Palladius, lib 1 tit 40 in fhewing the Method of making the hot Cells of the Baths, fays thus *Su penfinas vero cellarum fic facies, Aream primo bipedis fternis, inclinata fit tamen ftratura ad fornacem, ut fi pilam miferis, intro ftare non poffit, fed ad fornacem recurrat Sic evenict, ut flamma altum petendo, cellas faciat plus calere* And in the fame Chap. he fays, *Cameræ in balneis fi fignina fiant, fortiores funt, quæ vero de tabulis fiunt, virgis ferreis tranfverfis, & ferreis arcubus fuftinentur* To thefe two Paffages we are beholden for the full Explanation of thefe Words, and from thence we may conclude that thefe Words are rightly written, which the Difficulty of un-derftanding them had given fome caufe to doubt

17 *Cœnatio*] This feems to have been a leffer Room than the *Triclinium* or *Œcos*, though defign'd for the fame ufe, only the former were for greater Entertainments, and this for more private conftant Meals, and it was fo call'd from that which was eat there, which (if they had two in a Day) was however in the Evening, and their chief Repaft By the Defcription we meet with of thefe Rooms in fome Authors, it appears they were fometimes as large as the *Triclinia*, and probably both Words were fometimes indifferently ufed for the fame Room

18 *Procœton*] This Room and the *Amphithalamus*, mention'd by *Vitruvius, l 6 c 10* feem to have been almoft the fame, allowing that the *Thalamus* fignifies only a Marriage-chamber, or where a
married

bernum, est enim subductum omnibus Ventis. Huic Cubiculo aliud, & Procœton communi Pariete junguntur. ¹⁹ Inde Balnei Cella frigidaria, spatiosa & effusa, cujus in contrariis Parietibus duo Baptisteria, velut ejecta sinuantur; abunde capacia, si innare in proximo cogites. Adjacet Unctuarium, Hypocaustum, adjacet Propnigeon Balnei, mox duæ Cellæ magis elegantes quam sumptuosæ. Cohæret callida Piscina mirifice, ex qua natantes Mare aspiciunt. Nec procul Sphæristerium, quod callidissimo Soli, inclinato jam Die, occurrit.

for Height a Summer, but for its being fenced against the Weather, a Winter Room, for it is shelter'd from all the Winds. Joining to this Cubiculum is another, and a Procœton, with one common Wall. ¹⁹ Thence you enter the spacious and extensive Cella frigidaria of the Baths, in whose Walls opposite to one another are two Baptisteria, bending out into the Room, capacious enough to swim in, should you so incline, without going further. Joining to this is the Unctuarium, the Hypocauston, and Propnigeon of the Baths, and two more Cells, rather elegant than sumptuous. Fix'd to these by a more than ordinary Skill is the callida Piscina, from whence those that swim may have a Prospect of the Sea. At a small Distance is the Sphæristerium, which lies expos'd to an extreme warm Sun at the Decline of Day. Here

---

mon'd Couple lay, and *Caton*, or *Κοίτη*, a common Bed-chamber for single Persons. The Account *Turn* is gives of this Room is as follows. *Præsto idus autem dextra & sinistra cubiculi sunt collocata, quorum unum thalamus, alterum amphithalamus dicitur.* Where if *ample* be restrained to the common Signification of the Word, *viz. curton, or utrinque*, it will be difficult to find out the Disposition of these two Rooms, but if it be allow'd to be *Antithalamus*, this Passage will appear in a much clearer light. The only Difference between the *Antithalamus* or *Antiœcton of the Greeks*, and the *Procœton* of the *Romans*, seems to have been, that the first was a Room opposite to the Bed-chamber, and divided from it by a Passage, and the other was the Room before you come to the Bed-chamber, from which it was separated only by a Wall, though both the *amphithalamus* and *Procœton* were probably for the same use, viz. Bed-chambers for Servant.

19 *Inde Balnei, &* } For Explanation of all those Terms that belong to the Baths, the Reader is desir'd to examine the following Remarks on this Villa.

currit. Hinc [20] Turris erigitur, sub qua [21] Diætæ duæ, totidem in ipfa; præterea Cœnatio, quæ latiffimum Mare, longiffimum Littus, amœniffimas Villas profpicit. Eft & alia Turris: in hac Cubiculum, in quo Sol nafcitur conditurque, lata poft [22] Apotheca & [23] Horreum, fub hoc Triclinium, quod turbati Maris non nifi Fragorem & Sonum patitur, eumque jam languidum ac definentem: Hortum & Geftationem videt qua Hortus in-

Here arifes a [20] Turris, under which are two [21] Diætæ, as well as two in the Turris it felf; as alfo a Cœnatio, which has a very wide Profpect of the Sea, with its moft diftant Coaft, and feveral beautiful Villas. Befides this there is another Turris containing a Cubiculum, in which both the rifing and fetting Sun are beheld; behind this is an [22] Apotheca and [23] Horreum, underneath is a Triclinium, where never but in a Storm is heard the Roaring of the Sea, and then but faint-

C

---

[20] *Turris*] This was a Term of Fortification among the Antients, and fignify'd thofe Buildings that were commonly fet at proper Diftances in the Walls of their Cities, and raifed higher than the Walls themfelves. Their Form *Vitruvius* tells us, l. 1. c. 6. was commonly round or Polygonal, for the fake of Strength, but it is not to be queftion'd when they were imitated in private Architecture, as in this *Villa*, they were made after a more convenient Form. By this Paffage in *Pliny* it appears, that only that Part of the Building which was higher than the reft, was meant by the *Turris*.

[21] *Diætæ*] *Diæta*, fignifies an entire Appartment, that contain'd Rooms proper for all the common and daily Actions of Life, but did not always confift of any certain Number, or fame fort of Rooms, and this may be collected from feveral Paffages in in the two following Epiftles. This Word, fo often ufed by *Pliny*, feems to be the fame that fome Authors call *Manfio*, *Habitaculum*, or *Conclavium*, which latter, as *Feftus* witneffes, is fo call'd from being under one common Key.

[22] *Apotheca*] *Theca* fignifies a Repofitory, of which there were feveral about their *Villas*, and plac'd according as what they contain'd requir'd, and were fometimes nam'd from their particular Ufe, as the *Bibliotheca* from Books, *Pinacotheca* from Pictures, *Oporotheca* from Apples or other Fruit, but *Apotheca* feems, by the Ufe feveral Authors make of the Word, to have been a Repofitory that had no peculiar Office affign'd to it, and fometimes we find it fignifying a Wine-Cellar, which, however, could not be the Ufe which this of *Pliny's* was put to, fince it was one of the higheft Rooms in the Houfe, and quite feparate from all the other Offices and Rooms, and feems indeed, moft probably, to have been a Clofet for particular Rarities.

[23] *Horreum*] This fignifies that Place in the *Villa Fructuaria*, in which they laid up their Grain, and this Paffage fhews, that in thefe *Villæ Urbanæ* were retain'd the Names of Rooms proper to Farm-Houfes; for *Pliny* had no Land near this *Villa*, and confequently wanted no Granary, and by what he fays, l. 8. ep. 18. we may fee that *Horreum* was fometimes ufed to fignify a Repofitory for Works of Art, which was very probably the Office of this Room.

includitur ²⁴ Geſtatio Buxo, aut Rore marino ubi deficit Buxus, ambitur; nam Buxus, qua parte defenditur Tectis, abunde viret, aperto Cælo, apertoque Vento, & quanquam longinqua Aspergine Maris, mareſcit Adjacet Geſtationi, interiore Circuitu, Vinea tenera & umbroſa, nudiſque etiam Pedibus mollis & cedens Hortum Morus & Ficus frequens veſtit, quarum Arborum illa vel maxime ferax eſt Terra, malignior cæteris Hac non deteriore quam Maris Facie Cænatio remota a Mari fruitur; cingitur Diætis duabus à tergo, quarum Feneſtris ſubjicet ²⁵ Veſtibulum Villæ, & Hortus alius

faintly It looks on the Garden, and Geſtatio *that ſurrounds the Garden. The* Geſtatio *is encompaſs'd with Box, or Roſemary where the Box is wanting, for Box, where it is ſhelter'd by Buildings, flouriſhes much, but withers if expos'd to the Wind or Weather, or be in the leaſt ſubject to the ſprinkling of the Sea Water To the inner Circle of this* Geſtatio *is join'd a ſhady Walk of young Vines ſoft and yielding even to the naked Feet. The Garden is cover'd with Fig and Mulberry Trees, of which this Soil is fruitful, tho' not kindly to others This Proſpect, not leſs pleaſant than that of the Sea, is enjoy'd from a* Cænatio *diſtant from the Sea, it is encompaſs'd on the back with two* Diætæ, *whoſe Windows look on the* ²⁵ Veſtibulum *of the Villa, and another*

---

²⁴ *Geſtatio*] This ſeems to have been a principal Part in the *Roman* Gardens in *Pliny's* time It was uſed either for Riding, or being carried in their *Vehicula* Its Form was commonly Circular, or at leaſt in a great meaſure reſembled a Circus, as may be collected from *Pliny*, and from an antient Inſcription mention'd by *Gruter*, p 201 from which we may alſo obſerve, that theſe Places were laid out by meaſure, perhaps that they might know how many Miles they had gone, for that they took their exerciſe by Rule appears by what *Pliny* ſays of *Spurinna*, that he every Day rode juſt ſuch a Number of Miles, and this his Exerciſe was very probably taken in the *Geſtatio*, and computed by the times he had rode round it That they did not conſiſt only of one Path, may be concluded from what he ſays a little further in this Epiſtle, *Interiore Circuitu*

²⁵ *Veſtibulum*] What Part of the Houſe this was *Gallus*, from *Cæcilius Gallus*, tells us in theſe Words, *Veſtibulum non eſſ in ipſis Ædibus nec partem Ædium, ſed locum ante januam Domus per quem à via aditus acceſſumque eſt ad Ædes, in qua quidem inter viam & fores loco Salutatores & Clientuli Patronos præſtolabantur ut deducerent* As that Part of our Houſes which moſt reſembles the *Atrium* of the Antients is the Hall, ſo thoſe Porches or Colonades, that are before the Doors of ſome of ours, are the ſame with the *Veſtibula* of the *Romans*, and for the making of which perhaps there was formerly
(no

lius pinguior & rufticus. Hinc [26] Cryptoporticus prope publici Operis inftar extenditur; utrinque Feneftiæ, à Mari plures, ab Horto fingulæ, & altius pauciores: hæ, cum ferenus Dies & immotus, omnes; cum hinc vel inde Ventus inquietus, qua Venti quiefcunt, fine injuria patent: ante Cryptoporticum [27] Xyftus Violis odoratus, Teporem Solis infufi Repercuffu Cryptoporticus auget, quæ ut tenet Solem, fic Aquilonem inhibet, fummovetque; quantumque Caloris ante, tantum retro Frigoris: fimiliter Africum fiftit, atque ita diverfiffimos Ventos alium alio à latere

ther more rough and fruitful Garden. From hence a [26] Cryptoporticus *extends it felf, for Largenefs comparable to publick Buildings; on both fides are Windows, on that next the Sea are the greater Number, on the Garden fide they are fingle, and in the higher Row they are not fo many Thefe, when the Day is ferene and calm, are all open'd; but when the Wind is troublefome on either fide, thofe on the oppofite are open'd without any Inconveniency. Before the Cryptoporticus is a [27] Xyftus, fragrant with Violets, in which the Heat of the Sun is encreas'd by the Repercuffion of the* Cryptoporticus, *which at the fame time keeps off the North-Laft Wind, fo that as there is great Heat on one fide, there is as much Coolnefs on the other In like manner it ftops the South-weft; fo that the*

(no more than there is now) any fix'd Rule, but their Form was vary'd according to the Fancy of the Defigner. This *Veftibulum,* mention'd in this Epiftle, was probably that Part of the Oval Court which lay next to the *Atrium,* and was the firft Part of the Houfe that was enter'd It is by *Pliny,* in the Defcription of the Profpect from the *Triclinium,* call'd alfo a *Porticus*

[26] *Cryptoporticus*] This Room, as its Name fignifies, was an enclos'd or private *Porticus,* fo call'd to diftinguifh it from the *Porticus,* whofe Roof was only fupported by Pillars The Ufe of this Room was for the Exercife of Walking, when the Weather would not permit the Ufe of thofe Walks they had *fub dio,* and the Method they took to make it at all Seafons convenient, may be feen by the Defcription *Pliny* gives us of this

[27] *Xyftus*] This Term of Art cannot be better explain'd than by *Vitruvius's* own Words, *l 6 c 10 Xyftos enim Græca appellatione, eft Porticus ampla latitudine, in qua Athletæ per hyberna tempora exercentur Noftri autem hypethras ambulationes, Xyftos appellant, quas Græci Peridromidas dicunt* By this Account of it, and by what may be collected from *Pliny,* it feems to mean no more than an open Walk like our Terraces

litere frangit & finit. Hæc Jucunditas ejus Hyeme, major Æftate ante Meridiem Xyftum, poft Meridiem Geftationis, Hortique proximam Partem Umbra fua temperat, quæ, ut Dies crevit decrevitque, modo brevior, modo longior huc vel illuc cadit. ipfa vero Cryptoporticus tunc maxime caret Sole, cum ardentiffimus culmini ejus infiftit: ad hoc patentibus Feneftris Favonios accipit, tranfmittitque, nec unquam Aere pigro & manente ingravefcit. In capite Xyfti deinceps Cryptoporticus, Horti Diæta eft, Amores mei; re vera Amores ipfe pofui. In hac [28] Heliocaminus quidem, alia Xyftum, alia Mare, utraque Solem. Cubiculum autem Valvis, Cryptoporticum Feneftra profpicit quæ Mare contra Parietem medium Zo-

the Violence of the feveral Winds is broken by its different fides. Thefe Delights it affords in Winter, but greater in Summer; for before Midday the Xyftus, *in the Afternoon the* Geftatio *and neareft Part of the Garden is made temperate by its Shade, which, as the Day either encreafes or decreafes, wherever it falls is either longer or fhorter. The* Cryptoporticus *is then indeed moft free from Sun, when it fhines moft intenfly on its Roof. Add to this, by opening all the Windows it has a thorough Draught of the Weftern Breezes, nor ever is clouded by a thick ftagnated Air. At the head of the* Xyftus *jetting out from the* Cryptoporticus, *is the* Diæta *of the Garden, which I call my Delight; for truly there I have placed my Affections. In this is an* [28] Heliocaminus, *one fide of which looks to the* Xyftus, *the other to the Sea, and both to the Sun, from its Folding-doors is feen the* Cubiculum, *from the Windows the* Cryptoporticus; *on the fide that is next the Sea, and oppofite to the middle Wall, a very elegant*

---

28 *Heliocaminus*] This Word, if render'd according to its Etymology, will fignify a Sun-Chimney, but here I think it cannot mean more than a Room extraordinarily heated by the Sun, and is the fame that fome Authors call the *Solarium*

²⁹ Zotheca perquam eleganter recedit, quæ Specularibus & Velis obductis reductisve modo adjicitur Cubiculo, modo aufertur: Lectum & duas Cathedras capit, à pedibus Mare, à tergo Villæ, à capite Sylvæ, tot Facies Locorum, totidem Feneftris & distinguet & miscet. Junctum eft Cubiculum Noctis & Somni: non illud Voces Servulorum, non Maris Murmur, non Tempeftatum Motus, non Fulgurum Lumen, ac ne Diem quidem fentit, nisi Feneftris apertis: tam alti abditique Secreti illa Ratio, quod interjacens ³⁰ Andron Parietem Cubiculi, Hortique diftinguit, atque ita omnem Sonum media Inanitate confumit Applicitum eft Cu-

gant ²⁹ Zotheca *does as it were retire, to or from which, by opening the Windows and Curtains, a Cubiculum is either added or separated. This Zotheca contains no more than a Bed and two Chairs, from the Bed's Feet you have a Prospect of the Sea, from its back that of neighbouring* Villas, *and from the head you see the Woods, so many Windows affording so many Prospects, sometimes all seen at once, at other times separately. Joining to this is a* Cubiculum *for Night and sleep, for there I am not disturbed by the talking of my young Servants, nor by the Roaring of the Sea or Storms, neither is the Glare of Lightning, or even the Day perceiv'd, till the Windows are open'd This profound Silence is caused by an* ³⁰ Andron, *which divides the Wall of the* Cubiculum *from that of the Garden, so that all Noise is drown'd in the void Space that lies*

D   *between*

---

²⁹ *Zotheca.*] The Use of this Room, by the Description of those of *Pliny*, seems to have been for composing themselves in the Day-time, and by his Account there seems to have been two things in common to them, *viz* that they were no otherwise parted from the neighbouring Room but by Folding-doors and Curtains, and the other three Sides not being contiguous to any Building, there was in each a Window That these Rooms were but small appears by the little Furniture, which yet seem to fill those of *Pliny*.

³⁰ *Andron*] In the same Place, *viz. l 6 c 10* where *Vitruvius* has told what the *Roman Xyftus* was, he has explain'd the *Andron* in these Words, *Inter hæc autem Periftylia & Hofpitalia, itinera funt, quæ*

Cubiculo Hypocauftum perexigu-
um, quod angufta Feneftra fup-
pofitum calorem, ut Ratio exigit,
aut effundit, aut retinet. Procœton inde & Cubiculum porrigitur
in Solem, quem Orientem ftatim
exceptum, ultra Meridiem, obli-
quum quidem, fed tamen fervat.
In hanc ego Diætam cum me re-
cipio, abeffe mihi etiam à Villa
mea videor; magnamque ejus Voluptatem, præcipue Saturnalibus
capio, cum reliqua Pars Tecti Li-
centia Dierum, Feftique Clamo-
ribus perfonat · nam nec ipfe me-
orum Lufibus, nec illi Studiis meis
obftrepunt Hæc Utilitas, hæc
Amœnitas, deficitur Aqua falienti,
fed Puteos ac potius Fontes habet,
funt enim in fummo & omnino
Litoris illius mira Natura, quocunque Loco moveris Humum,
obvius

between Clofe to the *Cubiculum is
a fmall Hypocauftum, at which,
by means of a very fmall Window,
the Heat that lies under the Floor,
is either retain'd, or let out, at pleafure From thence a* Procœton *and
Cubiculum extend into the Sun,
from which latter the Sun is enjoy'd,
(tho' obliquely) from almoft its Rife,
till after Mid-day When I retire
to this Diætr, I fancy my felf ab-
fent from my* Villa, *and take great
Pleafure in it, efpecially in the time
of the* Saturnalia, *when the other
Parts of the* Villa *by the freedom
allow'd at thofe times, refound with
feftival Clamour for here I neither
hinder then Diverfions, nor they my
Studies Thefe Conveniencies, thefe
Pleafures, are attended with the
want of falling Water, which yet
find a fupply from natural Wells or
rather Springs, for they lie near the
Surface thro' the whole Coaft there
is this wonderful Quality, that
wherefoever you ftir the Earth, you
readily*

---

que *Mefaule dicuntur, quod inter duas Aulas media funt interpofita, noftri autem eas Andronas appellant* The two *Aule that this Andron, or Paffage, lay between, is has been before obferved, were the fame with the* Roman Catedra, *and probably in time this Word* Andron *came to fignify a Paffage between other Places as well as Courts, as appears by this mention'd by* Pliny *to part the Building from the Garden*

obvius & paratus Humor occurrit, isque sincerus, ac ne leviter quidem tanta Maris Vicinitate salsus Suggerunt affatim Ligna proximæ Sylvæ cæteras Copias Ostiensis Colonia ministrat Frugi quidem Homini sufficit etiam Vicus, quem una Villa discernit, in hoc Balinea meritoria tria, magna Commoditas, si forte Balineum domi, vel subitus Adventus, vel brevior Mora calefacere dissuadeat Litus ornant Varietate gratissima, nunc continuo, nunc intermissa Tecta Villarum, quæ præstant multarum Urbium Faciem; sive ipso Mari, sive ipso Litore utare. quod nonnunquam longa Tranquillitas mollit, sæpius frequens & contrarius Fluctus indurat Mare non sane preciosis Piscibus abundat; Soleas tamen & Squillas optimas suggerit Villa vero nostra etiam mediterraneas Copias præstat, Lac in primis; nam illuc è Pascuis Pecora conveniunt, si quando Aquam, Umbramve sectantur Justisne de Causis eum tibi videor incolere, inhabitare, diligere

readily and easily find Water, and that perfectly good, and not in the least brackish tho' so near the Sea The neighbouring Woods afford Fuel in abundance And other Conveniencies may be had from Ostia To a frugal Man what a Village affords, that is only separated from me by another Villa would be sufficient; in this Place are three publick Baths, which is a great Conveniency, if by my at any time unexpected Arrival, the Bath of my House is unprepar'd, or my short Stay does not give opportunity for it The Shore is adorn'd with a grateful Variety, by Prospects of Villa's, sometimes seemingly join'd together, and at other times farther asunder; which exceeds the Prospects of many Cities; whether you travel on the Sea or Shore Which sometimes is soften'd by a long Calm, but is more often harden'd by the contending Waves The Sea indeed does not abound in choice Fish; yet it produces Soles and the best Prawns My Villa even exceeds in the Plenty of the inland Country, principally in Milk, for thither the Cattle come from their Pasture, when they seek Water and Shade. Judge you whether I have

not

ligere Seceſſum ? quem tu, nimis urbanus es, niſi concupiſcis: atque utinam concupiſcas, ut tot tantiſque Dotibus Villulæ noſtræ maxima Commendatio ex tuo Contubernio accedat !

Vale.

not cauſe to continue, and delight in this Retirement ; which were you not too fond a Lover of the City you would your ſelf covet And I wiſh you did, that by your Participation in the Pleaſures of it a greater than any its other Commendations might be added to my little Villa !

Farewel.

REMARKS.

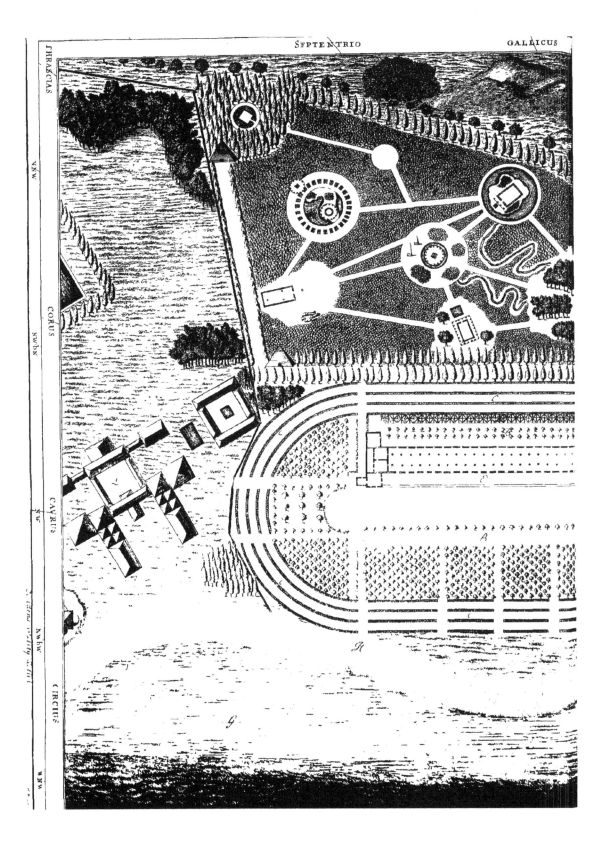

SEPTENTRIO   GALLICUS

THRASCIAS

NNW

CORUS

NWbN

CAVRVS

NWbW

CIRCIVS

WNW

SUPERNAS   AQUILO   BOREAS

CARBAS

SOLANUS   EAST

ORNITHIAE   ESE

CÆCIUS   ENE

EURUS   SE

VULTURNUS   SSE

LAURENTINUM

A Atrium
B Hortus
C Gestatio
D Vinea
E Xystus
F Hortus pinguis & Rusticus
G Mare
H Littus
I Gymnasium
K Sylvæ & Montes
L Villa vicina

a Equilia
b Tecta Vehiculis
c Lignarium
d Fœnile
e Piscinæ duæ
f Cellæ Servorum

REMARKS

ON

LAURENTINUM.

MOST of thofe *Roman* Authors who have wrote on Agriculture, have not thought it foreign to their Subject to take fome notice of *Villas* and their proper Situations; and from them it may be collected that the Antients efteem'd four Things effential to that of a good one, *viz* good Roads for themfelves and Carriages, or the Conveniency of a navigable River; next, fertile Land to produce what was neceffary for the Support of Man and Beaft; wholfome Water; and, laftly, an healthy Air; which laft-mention'd, as it immediately regarded the Life of the Inhabitant, was chiefly to be confidered · And tho' they have left us no Rules by which we fhould form our Judgment, they all agree that the Air next to a murfhy Soil is remarkably bad, and to be carefully avoided Though it was impoffible by any Art to cure the bad Airs of an ill-chofen Situation, yet *Varro, l 1 c 5 de Re Ruftica,* intimates, that the Skill of the Architect may in great meafure guard againft thofe that were but occafionally fo; and tells us how feveral Cities in *Greece* were preferved by *Hippocrates,* during a Peftilence, and of great Cures done by himfelf in a parallel Cafe at *Corcyra,* by no other Knowledge than that of rightly difpofing the Apertures of the Houfes. *Vitruvius* imputes the accidental Unhealthinefs of a Situation (fuppofing the Water always good, and the Building fo placed as not to be incommoded by Fogs) to proceed from the Sun or Wind, and

E   has

has spent the greater Part of *cap* 4, & 6 *l* 1 in giving Rules to guard against the Inconveniencies, and at the same time receive the Benefits, of both, *lib* 6 *cap* 1 in which he treats wholly on Private Buildings. The same Author says that the Fronts of all Buildings should be placed conformable to their Climate, as those of cold Countries (where there is seldom any Inconveniencies arising from too much Heat) the principal Part should be turned to the *South*, and in Buildings placed in a more *Southern* Latitude, where the Sun may have sometimes too great Power, the Front should be turn'd to the *North* And in this Book too, *cap* 9 he refers us to the same Rules for situating *Villas*, which in *lib* 1 he has laid down concerning Cities As to those Cities that were founded on an Inland Situation, if they had any principal Front, the Rules before-mention'd for different Situations in different Climates, was probably by him thought sufficient to direct the Architect in the Plan of the City, but left at the same time it should be thought that Rule might hold good with relation to Cities plac'd on the Sea-Coast, whose principal Front commonly fac'd the Sea, he informs us, *lib* 1 *cap* 4 that those in the Latitude of *Italy*, which fronted either to the *West* or *South*, must necessarily be unhealthy, because in Summer those to the *South* grow hot when the Sun rises, and at Mid-day are scorch'd with Heat, and those to the *West* at Sun-rising begin to be warm, at its full Meridian are intensly hot, and even at its Declension glow, so that those sudden Changes from one Degree of Heat to another, injure the Health of the Inhabitants Besides, says he, it may be observed, that the Bodies of Persons enfeebled by Heat in the Summer, recover their Strength and Health in Winter; for which reason he is entirely averse to placing their Buildings with their Fronts opposite to those Points from whence the hot Winds blow The Advantage that arises from proper Situations appears by what he says afterwards, concerning Cities founded in Marshes, which in the former Part of this Chapter he condemns as unhealthy, but here tells us that even these may be render'd healthy, by the Buildings being plac'd *North*, or *North-East* of the Sea, provided the Marshes lie so much higher than

the

the Surface of the Sea, that Drains may be made for the Water to run off, and at fome times the Flux of the Sea may enter them, and deftroy thofe *Animalcula* that are engender'd by Heat in ftagnated Waters, and being drawn in by the Breath together with the Air, were efteem'd the Caufe of many Diftempers. In this Chapter *Vitruvius* only fpeaks with relation to the Sun; but in the fixth of the fame Book he lets us know, that as many and great Inconveniencies may alfo happen from not difpofing the Plan of a City or Building fo as to avoid the ill effects arifing from inclement Winds, which he directs us by all means to exclude the Streets of a City, and gives a remarkable Inftance of the Inconveniences that *Mitylene* labour'd under through the Founder's Ignorance of this Rule, in which City, when the *South* Wind blew, it caufed Sicknefs by its great Heat. When *Corus* (which is a Point between *N N W* and *N.W* by *N* and is there a moift Wind) blew, the Inhabitants were troubled with Coughs, and when the *North* Wind blew, they recovered their former Health; but then it was fo cold, they could not bear ftaying long in the Streets. And a little further he tells us, that the fhutting out fuch Winds from a City not only preferved the Healths of found Perfons, but even cured thofe affected with Diftempers arifing from other Caufes, which in other Places requir'd the help of Medicines. This Caution being therefore thought of fuch confequence, *Vitruvius* has fpent the remaining Part of this Chapter in fhewing the Method of placing a City fo, that no Opening fhould be exactly oppofite to any of their twenty-four Points, or Winds. *Columella* and *Palladius*, where they have had occafion to fpeak of the Situation and Difpofition of *Villas*, feem to have been beholding to this Author for moft they have wrote on that Subject; and fince it may from thence be conjectur'd that his Works gave Laws to the *Roman* Architects, after him it may not be improper to take notice, how the Builder of the *Villas* of *Pliny* has obferv'd his Rules, where vary'd from them, and where proceeded upon Grounds for which we have the Authority of no extant Writer: But it may not be amifs, firft, to obferve, that the *Villa* of *Laurentinum*, whofe *Examen* we fhall firft enter upon, was not a Manfion sion House, round which *Pliny* had a large Estate, and all manner of Conveniencies for Life upon his own Ground, nor was it a Seat which he liv'd in it all Seasons, but where he spent only those Hours he had at leisure from the Business of the City, and as he himself tells us, *lib* 9 *cap* 40 he pass'd some time during Autumn and Winter; and whereas he also tells us, *lib* 4 *ep* 6 he possess'd nothing but the House and Gardens, nor diverted himself otherwise than by studying, for which reason, *lib* 1. *cp* 9 he calls this *Villa*

This Seat is by *Pliny* describ'd under three Heads, *viz* *Gratiam Villæ,* *Opportunitatem Loci, & Littoris Spatium*. The first of which relates to the Disposition of the House and Gardens, and the other two to the Situation, which he here considers with regard to its Pleasure, as well as Conveniency. In speaking of the Conveniencies of another *Villa* of the same Nature with this, *lib* 1 *cp* 4 he reckons as good Qualifications, *Vicinitatem Urbis, Opportunitatem Viæ, Mediocritatem Villæ, Modum Ruris*. Nor will it be found upon examination, that those of this his own *Villa* are different from these. It would have been superfluous for him, in a Letter to *Rome*, to have spoke any thing of the healthful Air of a Place in the Neighbourhood of *Ostia*, but at the end of this Epistle he gives us an account of the Goodness of the Water of that Place, which, as well as the Air, equally contributed towards the Health of the Inhabitant. But as he has not thought fit to speak of most of the Conveniencies and Pleasures of the Situation till after he has describ'd his *Villa*, we shall in our Remarks follow the same Method. The only Conveniency which he mentions before he comes to the *Villa* it self, is the Road to it, which he first considers with respect to its convenient Distance from *Rome*, which being, as he observes, but seventeen Miles, after having finish'd the Business of the Day in the City, he could very well arrive there before Night

Utrinque excipit, &c] The Inconveniency of this Road's being heavy to Carriages little affected him, who could bring whatever he wanted

from

from *Rome* to his *Villa*, by Water; and being fandy was no ill Quality in it, to a Perfon that only travelled it in Winter

Varia hinc atque inde Facies, &c.] Befides the fore-mention'd Advantages, the pleafant Views that were on each fide this Road might very properly be taken notice of, which made the Way lefs irkfome to the Traveller; and what he fays afterwards about the Cattle may ferve to confirm what has been before obferv'd, that he only fpeaks of the Advantages that relate to the Winter

Having defcrib'd the Road, he at length, as it were, arrives at the *Villa* it felf, and immediately proceeds to give us the Difpofition of all its Parts, without firft taking any notice on what Ground the *Villa* was plac'd, and to what Point the Front was turned : But as thefe are material towards underftanding feveral Paffages in the Difpofition, as alfo to prove the Judgment of the Builder, we fhall not here pafs them over without endeavouring to fhew what they might probably be.

By the Account *Pliny* has given us, at the end of this Epiftle, of the Ground on which this *Villa* was plac'd, and in particular to its being fubjected to Water, though that Water was good, yet, as it was not running Water, it might probably be unwholfome in the Heats of Summer, like that of a marfhy Situation, for this reafon, according to the Directions of *Vitruvius* in Cafes of the fame Nature, the Spot of Ground on which this Houfe was plac'd, muft have been *North-Eaft* of the Sea, and doubtlefs the other Cautions he has given about Drains were alfo obferv'd, fince the Ground lay higher than the Sea   As to what Point the Houfe fronted, (from feveral Paffages in the following Parts of this Epiftle, efpecially in fpeaking of the *Triclinium* next the Sea, to the Foundation of which he fays the Wind *Africus,* i e. the *South-Weft,* forced the Waves, and as it plainly appears that this Dining-Room was the fartheft from the Front of the Houfe, and directly oppofite to it) we might reafonably conclude that this Houfe fronted full *North-Eaft,* if

F

fion Houfe, round which *Pliny* had a large Eftate, and all manner of
Conveniencies for Life upon his own Ground, nor was it a Seat which
he liv'd in at all Seafons, but where he fpent only thofe Hours he had
at leifure from the Bufinefs of the City, and as he himfelf tells us, *lib*
9 *cap* 40 he pafs'd fome time during Autumn and Winter, and
whereas he alfo tells us, *lib* 4 *ep* 6 he peffefs'd nothing but the Houfe
and Gardens, nor diverted himfelf otherwife than by ftudying, for
which reafon, *lib* 1. *ep* 9 he calls this *Villa*

This Seat is by *Pliny* defcrib'd under three Heads, *viz* *Gratiam Villæ,
Opportunitatem Loci, & Littoris Spatium* The firft of which relates to
the Difpofition of the Houfe and Gardens, and the other two to the
Situation, which he here confiders with regard to its Pleafure, as well
as Conveniency In fpeaking of the Conveniencies of another *Villa* of
the fame Nature with this, *lib* 1 *ep* 4 he reckons as good Qualifications, *Vicinitatem Urbis, Opportunitatem Viæ, Mediocritatem Villæ, Modum Ruris* Nor will it be found upon examination, that thofe of this
his own *Villa* are different from thefe It would have been fuperfluous
for him, in a Letter to *Rome*, to have fpoke any thing of the healthful
Air of a Place in the Neighbourhood of *Oftia*, but at the end of this
Epiftle he gives us an account of the Goodnefs of the Water of that Place,
which, as well as the Air, equally contributed towards the Health of the
Inhabitant But as he has not thought fit to fpeak of moft of the Conveniencies and Pleafures of the Situation till after he has defcrib'd his
Villa, we fhall in our Remarks follow the fame Method The only
Conveniency which he mentions before he comes to the *Villa* it felf, is
the Road to it, which he firft confiders with refpect to its convenient
Diftance from *Rome*, which being, as he obferves, but feventeen Miles,
after having finifh'd the Bufinefs of the Day in the City, he could very
well arrive there before Night

Utrinque excipit, &c] The Inconveniency of this Road's being heavy
to Carriages little affected him, who could bring whatever he wanted
from

from *Rome* to his *Villa*, by Water, and being fandy was no ill Quality
in it, to a Perfon that only travelled it in Winter

Varia hinc atque inde Facies, &c] Befides the fore-mention'd Advantages, the pleafant Views that were on each fide this Road might very
properly be taken notice of, which made the Way lefs irkfome to the
Traveller; and what he fays afterwards about the Cattle may ferve to
confirm what has been before obferv'd, that he only fpeaks of the Advantages that relate to the Winter

Having defcrib'd the Road, he at length, as it were, arrives at the
Villa it felf, and immediately proceeds to give us the Difpofition of all
its Parts, without firft taking any notice on what Ground the *Villa* was
plac'd, and to what Point the Front was turned · But as thefe are material towards underftanding feveral Paffages in the Difpofition, as alfo to
prove the Judgment of the Builder, we fhall not here pafs them over
without endeavouring to fhew what they might probably be

By the Account *Pliny* has given us, at the end of this Epiftle, of the
Ground on which this *Villa* was plac'd, and in particular to its being fubjected to Water, though that Water was good, yet, as it was not running
Water, it might probably be unwholfome in the Heats of Summer, like
that of a marfhy Situation, for this reafon, according to the Directions
of *Vitruvius* in Cafes of the fame Nature, the Spot of Ground on which
this Houfe was plac'd, muft have been *North-Eaft* of the Sea, and
doubtlefs the other Cautions he has given about Drains were alfo obferv'd, fince the Ground lay higher than the Sea As to what Point the
Houfe fronted, (from feveral Paffages in the following Parts of this
Epiftle, efpecially in fpeaking of the *Triclinium* next the Sea, to the
Foundation of which he fays the Wind *Africus*, i e. the *South-Weft*,
forced the Waves, and as it plainly appears that this Dining-Room was
the fartheft from the Front of the Houfe, and directly oppofite to it) we
might reafonably conclude that this Houfe fronted full *North-Eaft*, if

I   we

we could suppose the Architect was unacquainted with the Inconveniencies that must attend a Building that fronted any principal Wind; and
since the Wind *Africus* might as well have driven the Waters to the
Door of the *Triclinium*, though placed betwixt that and another Point,
it is not improbable, but that the principal Entrance in the Front of
this *Villa* opened betwixt *Aquilo & Supernas*, which not at all contradicts
what he here says of the *Triclinium*, and afterwards of the *Cryptoporticus* By what has been observed from *Vitruvius*, that a City or Villa
seated on the Sea, should not have its principal Parts turned either
Southward or *Westward*, it may be objected, that the placing of this Villa
is absolutely contrary to Rule, but if it be again observed that the Inconveniencies which he mentions to proceed from such a Situation, are
only during the Heats of Summer, and that he seldom went to this Villa
but in colder Seasons, this warm Situation was an Advantage to it, besides,
by being so placed, and the Front of the House being almost *North-East*,
this Back Part (which was wholly allotted to the Master's Use) was by
those means sheltered from the colder Quarters, and though placed near
the Water (since none but warm Winds blew that way) did not at all
suffer by them

Villa Usibus capax, non sumptuosa Tutela] By this Beginning he
seems to prepare us for the Description of an House that contained nothing in it more than what was absolutely necessary, and not that of a
magnificent Villa, like that of *Lucullus*, or others of his own Time; a
Place rather proper for Study, and to retire to with a few select Friends,
than for State and Shew

Cujus in prima Parte Atrium, frugi, nec tamen sordidum] The
Office of this Part being for Servants or Clients to wait in, could not
properly be any where so well placed as near the Entrance of the House;
and, by his Description of this Court, he seems to hint, as if it was
customary for them very much to adorn those Parts which lay immediately before the House, which would have been very improper in him to
have

have done, had he not refolved equally to adorn all the reft of the Villa, and wou'd have been contrary to the *Decor* requir'd in all Buildings, as *Vitruvius* tells us, *lib* 1. *cap* 2 in thefe Words: *Ad confuetudinem autem Decor fic exprimitur, cum Ædificiis interioribus magnificis item Veftibula convenientia & elegantia erunt facta Si enim interiora Perfectus habuerint elegantes, Aditus autem humiles & inhoneftos, non erunt cum Decore*

Deinde Porticus, &c] In the City Houfes of the *Romans,* between the *Atrium* and the inner Court, there was ufually a Room call'd the *Tablinum,* mention'd by *Vitruvius, lib* 6 *cap* 4 This *Porticus* lay betwixt this *Atrium* and the *Cavædium,* though perhaps by being of another Form it is here call'd by another Name The Reafon for his giving it this round Form, may be upon two Accounts: Firft, to give a greater Grace to its Proportion, and to make the Fore-Part of it ferve for a more beautiful *Veftibulum* to the houfe, as it is afterwards call'd in this Epiftle; and in the next place, as being defign'd for a Shelter in tempeftuous Weather, it the better broke the Force of thofe Winds that blew on that fide, than if it had been more fquare The *Atrium* before-mention'd being only an open Court, it was neceffary that thofe who waited there fhould have fome Place of Shelter in bad Weather, which feems to have been the principal Caufe of making this *Porticus*; and to render it ftill the more fafe againft ftormy Weather, it was fecur'd with Glafs-Windows, and fhelter'd by an extraordinary Projection of the Roof The Provifion he had made for himfelf and Familiars, to walk in it all Seafons in the *Cryptoporticus,* may ferve to prove that this Place was not efteem'd for private Ufe; befides every body was neceffarily to pafs through it to the *Cavædium* By the Character of *feftiva,* which he gives to the *Area* of this round Court, it feems as if the Pavement had been adorn'd, and that perhaps with *Mofaick* Work, and, in his Opinion, mafterly done, fince he no where makes ufe of this Epithet, but to exprefs what he judg'd a Mafter-piece of Art or Nature, as appears by giving it to a fine Statue of an old Man, which he defcribes, *lib* 3 *cp* 6 and in fpeaking of a beautiful Girl, *lib* 5 *cp* 16. I ft

Est contra medias Cavædium hilare] *Vitruvius, lib* 6 *cap* 8 tells us, that the *Cavædium*, and those Places which were to be passed through in the way to it, were common to all Persons, and *Pliny*, in the Description of both his Villas, first describes these publick Places before he takes notice of the more private, as being the first Parts that offer'd themselves to view, and round, or adjoining to which, were commonly placed their Rooms for more private Use. The Epithet *hilare*, which he here gives this Court, and afterwards to the *Apodyterium* of *Tuscum*, might not improbably be upon the Account of its Ornaments of Architecture or Sculpture.

Mox Triclinium satis pulchrum, &c] Passing through the *Atrium*, *Porticus*, and *Cavædium*, as through a magnificent Avenue, he leads us to this Dining-Room, which, being as it were the Head of the House, he thought proper to take notice of before the lesser Members. The Description he gives of this Room, in a great measure answers that of the *Cyzican Triclinium*, mention'd by *Vitruvius, lib* 6 *cap* 6 and tho' not turn'd, like that, to the Garden, yet its Folding-Doors and Windows afforded as beautiful natural Prospects, which our Author seemed to prefer to those of Art. It may indeed be reasonably objected, that as *Laurentinum* was a Winter Villa, this Room seems to have been too open, and exposed to the Weather, and certainly it was so. To remedy which Inconveniency, he had another more proper at such Seasons (as shall be taken notice of in its Place.) At the same time this seems extremely well disposed to enjoy all the calm, Sun-shiny Days in Winter; for though there were such Openings, yet, as it stood almost *South-West*, and was guarded from all other Winds but those that blew from warm Quarters by the Jettings-out of some Parts of the Villa, it must have received all the Heat of the Sun, and have been very little incommoded by sharp Airs. Though it was their Custom to adorn this principal Room in the most costly manner, with Paintings, Marble, *&c.* yet, as at the Beginning of this Description he seems to affect a simple rather

than

AUSTER   LIBONOTUS

SOLANUS

AQUILO

a   Vestibulum et Ostium
b   Porticus
c   Area
d   Cavædium
e   Triclinium
f   Cubiculum amplum
g   Cubiculum minus
h   Cubiculum cum Apoda-
    ...ratum
i   Transitus
k   Dormitorium
l   Cænaculum p... depunum
m   Cas...
n   Culc...
o   Bract...
p   Cubiculum ab...
q   Camera
r   Cella ...daria
s   Archiarium
t   Hypocaustum
u   Propnigeon
w   Baptisteria duo
x   Duæ Cellæ
y   Sphærosterium
z   Triclinium

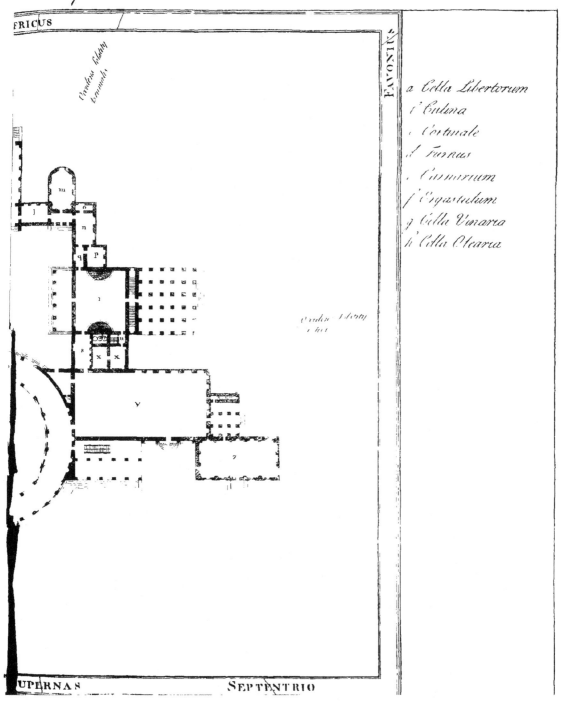

FRICUS

FAVONIUS

SUPERNAS   SEPTENTRIO

a Cella Libertorum
b Culina
c Cortinale
d Furnus
e Carnarium
f Ergastulum
g Cella Vinaria
h Cella Olearia

thin a fumptuous Manner, he thought he fhou'd vary from the *Decor*, if this Room fhou'd have been fo adorned, as to deferve a better Epithet than that of *fatis pulchrum*, which he here gives it. This Room had alfo two Profpects, one of the Water, and the other of the Land ; the former of which was three times repeated from fo many fides of the *Triclinium*, the latter, from the Door of the *Triclinium*, was feen through the Houfe, which was here a double Benefit to it, for thofe Parts of the Houfe it felf, which were feen, being the moft adorned, became Part, and added to the Beauty of the Profpect, and lying *North-ward* of that Room, at the fame time kept off thofe cold Winds.

Hujus a læva, &c] From the *Triclinium*, he proceeds next to give an account of what lay *Eaft* of it ; and this, though not called fo, feems to have been the Mafter's own *Diæta*, which, as may be alfo obferved in *Tufcum*, is the firft *Diæta* he defcribes. This Part of the Houfe confifted of four Rooms, three of which feem to have been Members of his own Appartment.

Cubiculum eft amplum] It has been before obferved in the Notes upon this Epiftle, and endeavoured to be proved, that *Cubiculum* did not only fignify a Bed-Chamber, but was a common Appellation for all but the principal Rooms in the Houfe, fuch as thofe for bathing and eating, and it may be alfo obferved that, adjoining to every *Triclinium*, but one that he defcribes in both Villas, was a *Cubiculum*, as a Withdrawing-Room, either for the Guefts to ftay in till the Tables were covered, or for the Servants that were neceffary to attend in during the Meal ; for this Reafon, and that it might bear fome Proportion to the *Triclinium*, this Room was of courfe to be large.

Deinde aliud minus, &c] It is neceffary to take notice, that wherever our Author mentions the rifing or the fetting Sun in either Villa, if he is defcribing a Winter Room, he then fpeaks of the Sun as confidered in that Seafon, and *vice verfa* ; and as the Part he is now defcribing was

G   a Wina Winter Appartment, therefore the Windows he speaks of here did not look full *East* and *West*, the Sun's Rising during the Winter Solstice in the Latitude this Villa stood, being something *South* of the *Roman* Wind *Cæcius* (or, to speak in the Saylors Term, *S E* by *E* a little *Easterly*, or about seventy Degrees *South* of the *East*, and setting about as many Degrees *South* of the *West*) the Position of this Room will answer what he says of it The Difference he makes betwixt one of the Windows admitting the rising, and the other retaining the setting Sun, though they both saw it equally, seems to be spoken here in Commendation of a Winter Room, that could, when proper, have a view of the rising, and be warmed by retaining the setting Sun, which it did by means of its Projection, and the Angle it caused, which is afterwards taken notice of Besides the Benefit of the Sun, he observes it had the same Prospect the *Triclinium* had of the Sea, and was less incommoded by it, because it lay farther from it, and had another Room betwixt it and the Sea.

Hujus Cubiculi & Triclinii, &c] It is remarkable how, in this Place and several others, he takes all Opportunities to enjoy the Sun, both within Doors and abroad Being obliged, upon several Accounts, to make Projections in this Building, that he might not let slip any Conveniency that offer'd, he here, upon the Shore, made his Domesticks exercise themselves to preserve their Health, for which Use this Place seems to have been particularly proper, being sandy, as the *Gymnasium* or Wrestling Place in the *Grecian Palæstra* always was, and also near the Sea, in which they cou'd wash when their Exercise was over ; and being at the same time warm, those who exercised naked were the less incommoded by the Season The Heat of this Place was occasioned, first, by the Point it was turned to, and then encreased by the Rays of the mid-day Sun's being pent in between two Buildings, which made it also proper for his Servants to sit or walk in at their leisure time during the Winter, since they had no Fires but where absolutely necessary, as in the Kitchen and Baths, or in the Master's Appartments That this was not a Place that either he or his Intimates warmed themselves in, or walked in during Winter, appears by what he afterwards says of the *Xystus* and *Cryptoporticus*, where he made all Provision for walking warmly in the coldest Season. The only Inconveniency that seems to have attended this *Hybernaculum* (and which at the same time may serve to prove that it was *sub dio*, and not a Winter Appartment) is, that being exposed to the *South*, the House afforded no Shelter from the Winds that blew from that wet Quarter, but that the Rain drove in upon them; but then it had this Conveniency, that no other Winds were admitted but those that blew from that warm, though moist, Region

Cubiculum in Aspida, &c.] The Form given to the Wall of this Room, seems founded upon an Opinion that, as this Place was made with a Design to receive the whole Benefit of the Sun, it could not so properly do it without being made like that Curve, which they had a Notion that Luminary made in surrounding the Earth, and which we are since satisfied that the Earth makes round that Body This, as well as the *Cubiculum* last-mentioned, seem to have been Day-Rooms belonging to this Appartment, and made proper to be enjoyed in different Seasons; the former of which seems the more proper for bad Weather, and this for calm Days when the Sun shone This Room seems, in some things, to resemble the Character he afterwards gives of the *Zotheca*; but as it has not all the Qualities of that Room, he does not give it that Name, neither does he call it a *Bibliotheca*, though, as he says, it was made partly like one, with Places for Books in the Walls, perhaps not thinking it large enough, nor stock'd with Books proper to a Room so called; neither does the Aspect of this Room answer what *Vitruvius* directs, *lib. 6. cap* 7 in such Cases, and its looking *South* and *West* must necessarily have had the Inconveniency of a Library turned that way.

Dormitorium Membrum, &c.] There is no other Room in either Villa called by this Name, but that where the Master lodged for a constancy:
Other

Other Bed-Chambers he does not at all diftinguifh, or call them *Cubicula Noctis & Somni*, and in *lib 1 ep 3 Cubicula nocturna*   This fleeping-ing Room is the only one that he choofes on the *Eaft* Side of the Houfe for his own proper Ufe, perhaps that it might have a Profpect of the morning Sun, as *Vitruvius, lib 6 cap. 7.* directs Rooms of this fort fhoud · Befides this Advantage, it had alfo what perhaps (as a Mafter of a Family) he thought a great one, that of being placed near his Servants, one of whom, *viz* his *Notarius,* feems, by what he fays, *lib. 9 ep. 36* to have been lodged near him; fo that there was no Occafion for a *Procoeton* to this *Diæta*   To remedy the Inconveniency that muft have attended this Room in Winter, by being placed in fuch a cold Corner, adjoining to it was what he calls *Tranfitus,* or a Paffage, by which means he heated it   The reafon why he had not an *Hypocaufton* under this Room, as under fome others, may probably be, becaufe in thofe the Perfon that was in the Room cou'd beft judge whether the Heat was too ftrong or not, and accordingly let the Air or Heat come in as was requifite : But this being a Bed-Chamber, and for Sleep, it was eafy for a Servant that was without to let in whatever Heat might be required, which he cou'd be a good Judge of in this Paffage, and either moderate or en-creafe it at pleafure, without difturbing the Perfon that was afleep. The Ufe of this *Dormitorium* being only for Sleep, there is no Notice taken either of the Sun, Air, or Profpect.

Reliqua Pars, &c] The remaining Part of this Side containing nothing but neceffary Offices and Lodgings for his Servants, is what he next de-fcribes; though it was needlefs to tell how every Member of them was turned, fince there were ftanding Rules, for the placing of each of which perhaps few were then ignorant.

Ex alio Latere, &c.] Having faid all he thought proper on the *Eaft* Side of the *Triclinium,* he proceeds *Weftward,* which Side takes up al-moft all the remaining Part of the Defcription, and which wholly belonged to the Mafters Part, or what *Palladius* and others call the *Præ-*

.   *torium,*

torium, alluding to that Part of the *Roman* Camp divided from the common Soldiers, and set aside for the Use of the General

Cubiculum politiffimum.] As on the other side of the *Triclinium* there was a Room he called *Cubiculum amplum*, so on this there was another called *Cubiculum politiffimum*, and which, in the Plan, must answer the other, and perhaps was for the same Use, only with this Difference, that by its Character of *politiffimum* it seems to have been better adorned, and for the Guests only; the other being for the Use of Servants, Comedians, Musicians, &c to wait in; besides its being thus convenient to the *Triclinium*, as it also stood next to the *Cœnatio*, it might be of the same Uses to that. The Epithet *politiffimum* must certainly be said upon account of its Decorations, but as to what Nature they were of we must remain in the dark: Nor does this Character at all destroy the *Decor* required in this Villa, for there may doubtless be as much Politeness shewn in judicious, simple Ornaments, as in the most costly and laboured Performances of Art

Cubiculum grande, vel modica Cœnatio, &c.] In the Description of this Room there are two Things worthy notice, *viz* its Size and Disposition It seems, by what he says of it, that the Rooms were proportioned according to their Use, so that a moderate Room for Meals, was equal to one of the largest Size design'd for other Use; the reason of which must have been to render them capacious enough for the Servants that waited at Table, for those that played on the Musick, or read Lyricks or Comedies during that time, which was as customary in these their lesser Eating-rooms, as it was to act in their larger, either at, or after, their Repasts In his Description of his *Tuscan* Villa, we find the *Cœnatio quotidiana*, or constant private Eating-room, close to, or Part of, his own *Diæta*, but in this it cou'd not well have been so, without destroying his two Day-rooms; for by *Vitruvius's* Directions, *lib* 6. *cap.* 7. the Winter Eating-room was to be turned so as to have a Prospect of the setting Sun, which this *Cœnatio* had thoroughly, and

H   by by his saying *plurimo Sole*, &c. it appears that this was so disposed. Besides the Advantage of Warmth, it, at the same time, received not only the Light of the Sun by direct Rays, but by Reflection from the Water, so that (being a Winter Room,) fewer Windows served to enlighten it

Post hanc Cubiculum, &c.] By joining a *Procœton* to this and the following *Cubiculum*, it seems as if they were both *Cubicula nocturna*, these *Procœtona* being only for Servants to lie in; and as they were placed in the principal Part of the House, and most convenient for Winter, it is probable they were Chambers for Guests that were only Visitors for a short time, since to those of his own Family he allows one whole *Diæta*, which contained three or four Rooms. By *Altitudine æstivum* it appears, that the general Rule *Vitruvius* gives, *lib 6 cap 3* concerning the Height of Rooms, was sometimes (when either Conveniency or Beauty required) not at all regarded; but that they made a Difference in Height betwixt those for Winter and Summer, the more lofty being cooler than the other, and had not this been guarded from all Winds, as he tells us it was, we may suppose this wou'd have had the Proportions answerable to a Winter Room; but since it was not so incommoded, and was a principal Bed-Chamber, it must have been more graceful by its Loftiness, and therefore had its true Proportion, which was, that the Height was answerable to half the Side and End of the Room added together. We may collect from several Passages in *Vitruvius* and *Palladius*, that the Antients adorned their Winter Rooms different from those of the Summer, that their Furniture might not be injured by the too frequent Smoak of Fires and Lamps. What he here says about *Munimentis hybernum* is afterwards explained by himself, and his Meaning is, that the Room was sheltered from the Winds, though not enclosed on all sides, as in a Court, and was only exposed to those gentle Breezes that blew from that Quarter which they called *Etesia*, to which these Windows were almost directly turned; and in the Description of the Situation of *Tuscum*, he distinguishes between *Venti* and *Auræ*

                                                                    Inde,

Inde, &c] The Cuſtom of bathing their Bodies all over in hot Water, which the *Romans* uſed but ſparingly during the Time of the Commonwealth, in that of *Pliny* was become ſo habitual, that they every Day practiſed it before they lay down to eat, for which reaſon in the City the publick Baths were extremely numerous, in which *Vitruvius, lib. 5. cap* 10 gives us to underſtand there were for each Sex three Rooms for bathing, one of cold Water, one of warm, and the other ſtill warmer, which are by *Palladius, lib.* 1 *tit* 40 called *Cellæ piſcinales,* and there were alſo Cells of three Degrees of Heat for ſweating, beſides which, beyond doubt, there was another Room, though not mentioned by *Vitruvius,* called the *Apodyterium,* as well as the *Hypocauſtum* and *Propnigeon,* to heat the Rooms and Water By the Deſcription the ſame Author gives of the publick Baths of the *Grecians, lib. 5 cap* 11 we learn, they were made after another manner; and to the fore-mentioned Members were added others for anointing and bodily Exerciſe, which, after *Vitruvius's* Time, were imitated in the *Thermæ* of *Rome,* and by ſeveral *Romans* in their private Baths, of which, before particular Notice be taken, it may not be from the Purpoſe to enquire into their Manner of uſing their Baths, in which though they might in ſome Circumſtances differ, yet it is certain they all agreed in bathing the laſt thing they did before they entered the *Triclinium;* for which we cannot have better Authority than *Pliny* himſelf ſpeaking of *Spurinna, lib* 3 *ep.* 1 and afterwards of his Uncle *Pliny, lib. 6. ep* 16 he ſays, *lotus accubat,* &c. and in *ep* 20 *mox Balineum, Cœna, Somnus.* What preceded their waſhing was then Exerciſe in the *Sphæriſterium,* prior to which it was their Cuſtom to anoint themſelves, as appears, *lib* 9. *ep.* 36 where accounting for the Manner of ſpending his Time in the Country, ſpeaking of that Part of it which he paſſed in the Baths, he ſays, *unguor, exerceor, lavor* As for the Sweating-rooms, though they were doubtleſs in all their Baths, we do not find them to have been uſed but upon extraordinary Occaſions. Theſe Baths containing ſo many Parts or Rooms for ſo many ſeveral Uſes, muſt neceſſarily have taken up a large Part of the Houſe, which

always

always where it could be contrived, was oppofite to the Winter's fetting Sun, (as *Vitruvius, lib. 6. cap* 7 directs) for the Conveniency of Light and Heat at the fame time they were ufed

Balnei Cella frigidaria, &c] Though it is evident from *Vitru-vius,* that both the *Romans* and *Grecians* had fettled Forms for their publick Baths, we may yet fuppofe every private Perfon followed his own particular Humour, in either adding, taking from, or altering the Difpofition of his own private Baths   In thofe two *Pliny* has defcribed it may be obferved, that the Architect has rather followed the *Grecian* than *Roman* Manner, by adding feveral Members that *Vitruvius* does not mention in his *Roman* Baths, two of which are called by *Greek* Names, viz   the *Apodyterium,* which feems to anfwer the *Ephebeum,* and the *Sphæristerium* the *Coryceum* ; the *Unctuarium,* though a *Roman* Appellation, was probably the fame with that which the *Grecians* called *Elothefium*   As for the other Members, they feem to have been common to the Baths of both Nations . By what can be collected from Authors it appears, that thefe private Baths confifted of feven Parts, viz. the *Apodyterium, Cella frigidaria, Pifcina* or *Cella pifcinalis,* the *Cella tepidaria* and *caldaria* for fweating, the *Unctuarium,* and *Sphæriste-rium,* befides the *Hypocauftum* and *Propnigeon,* fome of which Members ferved for two Ufes, and others were omitted, as may be feen in both thefe Baths ; for in this of *Laurentinum* the *Cella frigidaria* ferved for the *Apodyterium,* and in *Tufcum* there is no Room fet apart for the *Pifcina,* which is there placed in the Area of the *Cella frigidaria*   The *Apodyterium,* which was the firft Room of the Baths, where they undreffed themfelves, and to which they returned when they came from Exercife or Bathing, was, as has been before obferved, omitted in this Bath, perhaps upon account of a Refolution *Pliny* feems to fet out with in the Beginning of this Defcription, that there fhou'd be nothing but what was abfolutely neceffary, which he might think this was not, when the *Cella frigidaria* could fupply the Place of the *Apodyterium,* as well as that of the *frigida Lavatio,* to which, in their publick Baths, they

assigned

affigned two feveral Rooms; and though this Room of the third Degree of Heat was called *Cella frigidaria*, it was not from its being a colder Room than ordinary, but only fo in refpect to others; for being near the *Hypocauflon*, and having fometimes the *Pifcina* of hot Water in the *Area*, it could not but have been warm in fome Degree, and the Coolnefs it had muft have rather proceeded from its Size, and the Quantity of Air it admitted, than from any other Caufe   The principal Ufe of this Room feems, by its cold Bath and Air, to have been defigned to prepare the Bodies of thofe that had been in warmer Rooms, for their going into the open Air   The Reafon why he here calls it *fpatiofa & effufa*, might only intend its feveral Ufés, befides containing the two *Baptifteria*

Adjacet Unctuarium] The *Cella frigidaria* of this Bath had feveral adjoining Members.   On one fide were the *Unctuarium, Hypocauftum* and *Propnigeon*; the firft of which was that in which, after they came from the Undreffing-room, they anointed themfelves before they entered the *Sphariflerium*; for which Reafon it was here placed betwixt thofe two Rooms: And it was alfo placed not far from the *Hypocauftum*, that when they entered it in the Way to the *Sphariflerium*, their Bodies, by the Heat, might be the better prepared to receive the Oyls; and fome of the more delicate of them, after Wafhing, made ufe of Perfumes

Hypocaufton] It was never thought neceffary, in any of their Baths, to have more than one Fire, which was lower than the Floor of the Rooms, and could therefore warm both them and the Water

Propnigeon.] This Part, which *Vitruvius*, in his Defcription of the *Roman* Baths, calls *Præfurnium*, as being that Room which was immediately next the Mouth of the Furnace, feems to have been fomething like, and defigned for the fame Ufe as the *Tranfitus* next the *Dormitorium* in this Villa, *viz* to receive and temper the Heat before it was adminiftered to the Sweating-rooms, fo that from thence they might receive what

I

Degree

Degree of Warmth they thought proper; though, at the fame time, the Fire that heated the Water was not at all abated

Mox duæ Cella magis elegantes quam fumptuofa] Adjoining to the *Propnigeon* was the *Cella caldaria*, or hotteft Room in their private Baths, and next that was the *Cella tepidaria*, or Room of a lefs Degree of Heat It is likely that all thofe Sorts of Cells were (for the fame Reafon *Vitruvius* directs in the *Laconicum*, viz to let in Air at pleafure) enlightened from the Roof, except when Buildings were placed over them, as *Palladius* tells us Winter Appartments fometimes were From the fame Author, *lib. 1 tit* 40. two things may be learnt concerning thefe Cells, viz their Proportion, which, he fays, were in Length one Third more than in Breadth; and alfo how thofe Cells were fufpended in order to receive the Heat, which Paffage has been fufficiently difcuffed in the Note on *fufpenfus & tabulatus* It appears by what *Seneca* and other Authors tell us, that they were extremely profufe in the Ornaments of their Baths, and it feems as if they were particularly fo in thefe Cells, for though he has paffed over feveral other Parts without taking any notice of their Ornaments, thefe, he obferves, were elegantly adorned, and we may at the fame time take notice, that no Cuftom cou'd make him vary from the Rule of Simplicity he at firft laid down, and that he avoided all fumptuous Ornaments.

Cobæret callida Pifcina, mirificè ex qua, &c] Tho' they adorned the Walls, Ceilings and Floors of the other Parts of their Baths, it was on the *Pifcina* they beftowed the moft Art, and in which they feemed to take moft Delight In the *Cella frigidaria* of their private Baths they had feveral Veffels to wafh in, which, either from their Shapes or Offices, were called by different Names, as, particularly, the *Labrum*, from its Margin refembling a Man's Lip; the *Pelvis*, a Veffel to wafh Feet in, and the *Baptifterium*, in which they dipped the whole Body; and this laft was fometimes large enough to fwim in, as thofe in both his Villas were: But when they had a mind to fwim at large in warmer Water,

they

they entered the *Piscina*, a Bason so called, as its Size bore some Resemblance of a Pond. Some of these in their publick Baths (according to all accounts) were so very large, that it has been a Doubt how they could be well heated; nor does it appear how it could be done by the Method *Vitruvius* directs, *l 5 c* 10. where he tells us, the Way was by placing three brazen Vessels over the *Hypocauston*, one for hot, another for warm, and the other for cold Water; so that as the Water ran out of the hot Vessel it was supplied by the Vessel containing the warm, and that by the Water from the cold Vessel: For which Reason, if there was a continual Call for hot Water, unless the Vessels and Fire were extremely large, the cold Water that came in must cool the Water in the hot Vessels faster than the Fire could heat it, and consequently without waiting some time for hot Water the Baths must have been chilled; of which Inconveniency he was not ignorant, as appears by what he says immediately after: *Testudinesque Alveorum ex communi Hypocausi calefacientur,* by which he means the Arches under the Bason, which Arches receiving the Fire of the *Hypocauston,* the Water that was in the Bason might be the longer kept warm, but still, notwithstanding all these Precautions, they could not always have a Supply of warm Water. In the following Draught may be seen the Method *Vitruvius* speaks of for heating their Baths.

a Vasa Aliena una   c Baptisterium
b Hypocauston   f Cella Frigidaria
c Testudines Alvei   g Propnigeon
d Alveus

To make good the fore-mentioned Defect, when the *Thermæ* were built, which may be said to contain in them Lakes of warm Water, they were obliged to make use of other Means to warm the Water, as may appear from what *Seneca* says, *Nat. Quæst. lib 3 cap 24. Facere solemus Dracones & Miliaria & complures Formas, in quibus Ære tenui Fistulas struimus, per declive circumdatas, ut sæpe eundem Ignem ambiens Aqua per tantum fluat Spatii, quantum efficiendo Calori sat est Frigida itaque intrat, effluit calida* By this Passage it is evident, that the Water acquired its Heat by passing through the Fire in a brass Pipe, and must have been more or less hot, according to the Length of its Progress. It seems, by what *Seneca* says, that sometimes they made only a winding Pipe, without any other additional Vessel; which Pipe, from its Serpentine Form, was called *Draco* But it was thought the better Way, to receive the cold Water in a large Boiler before it entered the winding Pipes. These Vessels were probably of several Forms, and the Pipes were differently disposed, but that which seems to have been the Vessel generally approved of was the *Miliarium,* of which *Palladius, lib. 1. tit 40* gives us the following Description: *Miliarium vero plumbeum, cui Ænea patina subest, inter foliorum spatia forinsecus statuemus fornace subjecta, ad quod Miliarium fistula frigidaria dirigatur, & ab hoc ad solium similis magnitudinis fistula procedat, quæ tantum calidæ ducat interius, quantum fistula illi frigidi liquoris intulerit.* From this and the foregoing Passage of *Seneca* it may be collected, that the *Miliarium* was a Leaden Vessel of a large Circumference, the middle Part of which was open for the winding Pipe and for the Draught of the Fire to pass through This Vessel of Water that surrounded the Flame or Draught of the Fire, was also placed upon Part of the same Fire, and for that Reason was obliged to have the Bottom of it of Brass, as were also the Pipes.

The Form of this Engine, and other principal Parts belonging to their Baths, will be best understood by consulting the following Drawing.

The

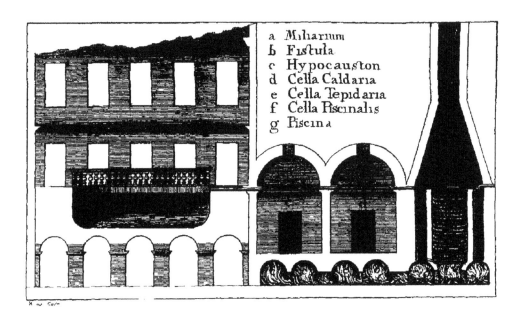

a Miliarium
b Fistula
c Hypocauston
d Cella Caldaria
e Cella Tepidaria
f Cella Piscinalis
g Piscina

The *Piscina* of uncommon Size probably had round them more than one of these Vessels, but those of a moderate Size might, without much Expence of Fire, have been sufficiently supplied from one, as from a Fountain of hot Water; so that there could be no Occasion to keep a Fire under the Bath, and they could have raised the *Piscina* from the Ground as high as the Top of the *Miliarium*, and the better make their *Balnea Penfiles* as luge as those on the Ground. The principal Pleasure proposed by those airy Baths was that of a Prospect while they were swimming, of which *Seneca, ep* 86 speaks thus *Blattaria vo-cant Balnea, si qua non ita aptata sunt, ut totius Diei Solem Fenestris amplissimis recipiant, nisi & laventur simul & colorantur, nisi ex Solio Agros & Maria prospiciunt.* *Pliny* too, in the Epistle before us, mentions the Prospect as the chief Commendation of the *Piscina* of this Villa, which he could not have enjoyed had it been upon the same Floor with the Cells; and it might be for the Reason of its being raised so much higher than the Ground, that he uses the Word *mirifice.* *Palladius, lib.* 1. *tit.* 40. says, the Lights of Summer Baths should be

K   oppofite

oppofite to the *North*, and thofe of Winter to the *South*, betwixt which Point and the *Weft* thofe of this *Pifcina* (that had a Profpect of the Sea) were turned.

Nec procul Sphariftcrium, &c] Having treated of thofe Parts of the Baths that were for anointing, fweating and bathing, he now comes to fpeak of that defigned for Exercife, which, though not really a Member of the Baths, was commonly joined to it, fince after the Exercife they there ufed, they immediately entered the *Pifcina*, to wafh off the Oils, Sweat and Duft contracted by the Violence of it; for which Reafon this Room and the *Pifcina* were commonly annexed to one another As this Room was generally in ufe towards the Clofe of the Day in Winter, and as they commonly exercifed naked, it was not improper to turn its Openings to the Sun at that Time

Hinc Turris erigitur, &c] Hitherto the whole Defcription, except that of the *Pifcina*, has been in *plano pede*, and probably for no other Reafon, than that by their being Winter Rooms they were therefore lefs expofed to the Wind: But as this Manner of Building, in fuch a flat Situation, would not admit from any Rooms (except thofe clofe to the Sea) a large Profpect, which was reckoned one of the greateft Pleafures of their Villas, it was requifite to raife fome Parts of the Houfe higher than the reft, nor could any be thought more proper than thofe in the Front, upon two Accounts; firft, as by their Height they fheltered all the lower and back Part from the bad Weather, and at the fame time added a grace to the Front, which would have been wanting to a Building that had confifted but of one Story. It may be obferved, that in this whole Defcription *Pliny* has taken fuch a Method, that he has not been obliged to pafs through one Room twice, and, in order to perfevere in it to the end, takes notice of this *Turris* that lay fartheft from the Gardens, referving the other till he is juft entering the *Geftatio*.

Sub

Sub qua Diæta dua, totidem in ipsa] The Rooms hitherto mentioned by *Pliny* have been only those belonging to his own Appartment, besides two principal Bed-chambers, and other Rooms that were in common to all that lodged on the Master's side of the House; but as these might not be sufficient for his Family, in this *Turris* he made four *Diæta*, which, by their Disposition, seem to have been more proper for Summer than Winter, unless secured from Cold by Fires, and making the Rooms proper for that Season: But it must be again observed, that though this was a Winter Villa, yet that he had taken care to enjoy the Pleasures of the Summer even here, appears by what he says of the *Cryptoporticus*

Præterea Cænatio, &c] This Room, 'tis evident by its Prospects, had its Windows turned the same way with the *Cænatio* before-mentioned, and must have been, like that, a Winter Dining-room: For though placed aloft, we do not find it had a view of the Woods and Mountains that lay *North-East* of the House; some other Rooms of the *Diæta* being probably on that side. The Reason of its being placed in the highest Part of the House must have been purely for the sake of Prospect; and we may particularly observe, that there is no Room in either Villa of whose Views he takes so much notice as of those for Meals; in all which he either describes the natural distant ones, or else the Works of Art that lay nearer. And hence we may perceive they endeavoured, while they were pleasing their Palates, to indulge their Sense of Seeing, as their Ears were pleased with the Musick which at the same time played. The Prospects mentioned from the *Triclinium*, were only that before the House, and that of the Sea behind it, the Jettings-out of the Buildings and its low Position obstructing the View of those which are mentioned here: But this Room, being so placed as to over-look the Garden and greater Part of the House, could on both sides command a large Prospect of the Coast and those Villas with which it was then well stocked; and also a much more extensive Prospect of the Sea.

Est

Eſt & alia Turris.] Either to preſerve the Uniformity of the Buildings, or that the other *Turris* could not contain all thoſe Rooms he
thought proper to be placed on high, muſt have been the Reaſon this
laſt was erected   And if this was of the ſame Size with the former, it
muſt have had in it more Rooms than are here mentioned but as four;
three or which were in the *Turris*, or higheſt Floor, and only one below under one of them

Cubiculum, in quo Sol naſcitur conditurque] The firſt he mentions in
the upper Story, was a Room that ſeems, like the *Cœnatio*, to be chiefly regarded for its Proſpect; and the Poſition anſwers, in all reſpects, that
Day-chamber of which he ſays, *Altera Feneſtra admittit Orientem*, &c
The Reaſon for altering his Phraſe in ſpeaking of this Room, might
proceed from its being placed ſo much higher than the other · For tho'
that admitted the riſing Sun, yet it was here ſooner ſeen, and at its firſt
Appearance above the Water; which he poetically calls its Birth, and
carries on the ſame Metaphor in deſcribing its Diſappearance in the Sea

In ſpeaking of the *Triclinium*, and the laſt *Cœnatio*, he has enume-
rated the beautiful Proſpects that, at all Times of the Day, could be
ſeen from thoſe two Rooms; but here he takes notice of one that ſur-
paſſed them all: And it was indeed a ſingular Advantage to the Proſpect
of this Room, which looking only on a large Body of Water, there was
ſomething wanting to terminate the View, the Eye being never pleaſed
with one that is unbounded; nor could it poſſibly have one more glo-
rious than the riſing and ſetting Sun, the moſt beautiful Proſpects in
Nature, at which Time only, or when the Moon, Ships, or diſtant Land
are ſeen, the Proſpect of the Sea can be truly ſaid to be agreeable. It is
certain, this Room had other Proſpects beſides theſe, but being of
an inferior Kind, and mentioned in other Places, they are here
omitted.

Lata

Floor of LAURENTINUM

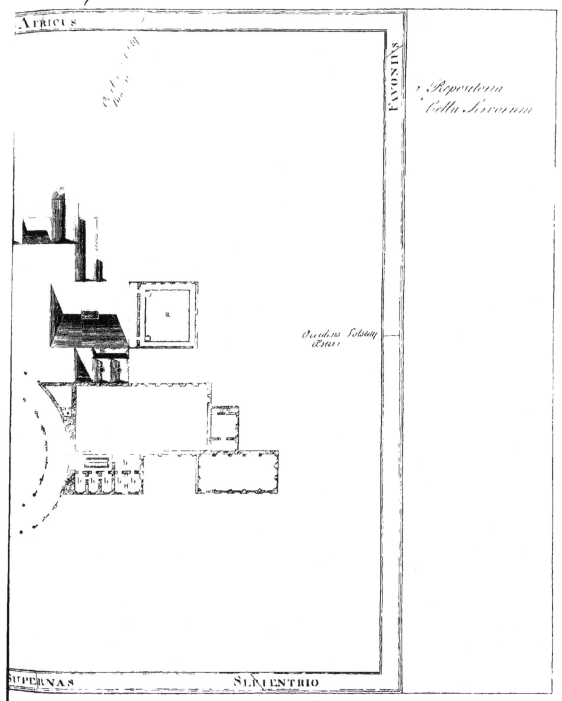

AFRICUS

FAVONIUS

Repositoria
Cella Servorum

Occidens Solstitij
Æstivi

a

b b b b b

SUPERNAS   SEPTENTRIO

AUSTER · LIBONOTUS

a *Linden Due*

b *the one little new*
mo ..

c *Curarlan, n ymor,*
ror..m . ottobiny

d *Spitio .*

e *Hin am*

Oreas al hu
trivia ob

Orecus Klong
Patra

VOLTURNUS

AQUILO

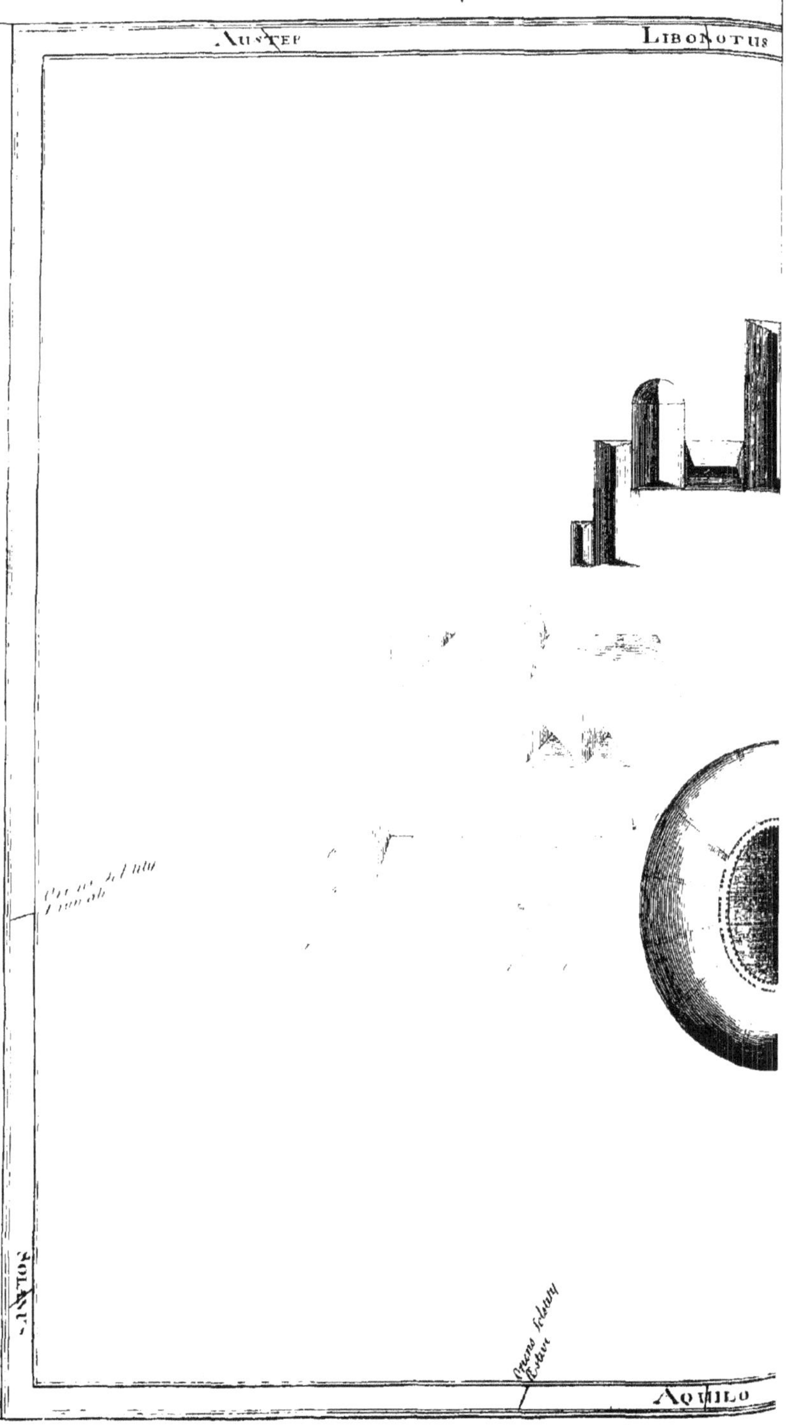

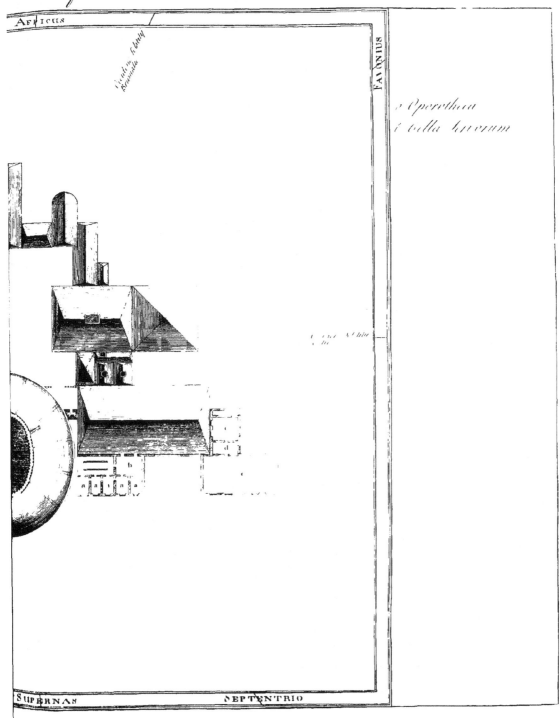

AFRICUS

FAVONIUS

SUPERNAS

SEPTENTRIO

Lata poft Apotheca & Horreum] What was the Ufe of thefe Rooms has been explained in the Notes on this Epiftle, and the former might be a Store-Room, in which they kept fuch things as they would preferve from the Damp, fince it could receive all its Air from the *Eaft*, and fhut out the *South* and *Weft*, which *Vitruvius, lib 6. cap* 7 calls moift Winds The *Horreum*, which was perhaps the fame with the *Pinacotheca*, was not only obliged to be turned from moift Quarters, but to have its Windows open to the *North*, that the Pictures and Works of Art, with which it was filled, might have a fteady true Light

Sub hoc Triclinium, &c] The former *Triclinium* was placed in fuch a manner, that in many Days it muft have been inconvenient in a Winter Villa fituated like this ∙ In order therefore to guard againft thefe Inconveniences, and that there might never be wanting a Room at all Seafons proper for the Reception of his Guefts, was this he now mentions contrived, from which, by its Pofition, could but juft, and that not unpleafantly, be heard the Roaring of the Sea, much lefs could it be incommoded by the Waves As the placing of it thus muft have taken from it all Profpects of the natural Face of the Country, it was therefore fo turned as to have a View of the Garden, where Art was the chief Beauty; in order to which it look'd *Weftward*, as Winter Dining-rooms were directed to do.

Geftatio Buxo, aut Rore marino, &c] In this Winter Villa it was thought needlefs to have large Pleafure-Gardens, for which reafon here were only thofe Places proper for Exercife, and common to all Villas, *viz* the *Geftatio*, the *Xyftus*, and another Walk, to which, being covered over at the top, he does not give the Name of *Ambulatio*. Thefe, with the *Area* the *Geftatio* furrounded, were all the Parts of which this Garden confifted.

The *Geftatio* was a principal Member near all their Villas, as appears from the mention he makes of four Gardens in feveral Epiftles, in each of which was one of those Places of Exercise What Sort of Place this was, and its Office, has been already spoken of in the Notes; and here it may not be improperly remarked, that it seems to have been their Custom to surround them with Box-hedges, wherever they would grow, as both this and that of *Tuscum* were, that they might in all Seasons have green Boundaries to their Ridings, and a Prospect over those Hedges as they rode along, which both in Winter and Summer might have been enjoy'd, without being incommoded with Cold or Heat; for the *Vehiculum* they were carried in was not open at the Top, like the *Currus*, and could be shut close on all sides, as appears, *lib. 7. cp 21 Tecto Vehiculo undique inclusus*

Vinea tenera & umbrosa, &c] While they were in the *Gestatio* they sometimes left the *Vehiculum*, and walked, and for that reason this Walk might be joined to it; which, by the Description of it, seems to have been like the covered Walk in one of the Pictures in *Naso's* Monument, and by its Character of *tenera & umbrosa*, we may suppose it more design'd for Summer or Autumn than Winter, when Shade was not wanted In an Account of the daily Exercises of *Spurinna*, mention'd, *l 3 cp 1.* amongst others, it was his Custom to walk naked when there was not too much Wind; and it is possible *Pliny* might have been so much pleased with the other's Method, as to have imitated him in it; for which reason the Softness of this Walk to naked Feet is here mentioned, which probably was occasioned by being covered with Sand, or set with the *Acanthus* he mentions in *Tuscum*

Hortum Morus & Ficus, &c] That Piece of Ground which was bounded by the *Gestatio*, and which he here calls the Garden, he thinks worthy of no other notice, than that it was planted with Fig and Mulberry-Trees, the Fruits of which, as well as of the Vines, were not ripe till his Time of coming to this Villa (in Autumn,) which, as well as the Nature of the Soil, might be one Reason for only planting these Trees. Though this seems to have been the same with our Fruit Gardens,

dens, yet was it here his principal Pleafure-Garden; and by diftin-
guifhing that which he mentions afterwards by the Character of *rufticus*,
we may think this was laid out after a better Form, to yield a more
agreeable View to thofe Rooms which had the Profpect of it

Within this Garden was a large Building, which, by fome Paffages, we
may fuppofe to have been joined to the main Houfe, and by other as con-
vincing Reafons feems to have been at fome fmall Diftance from it; but
be that as it will, it makes no material Alteration in the Difpofition or
Ufe of thofe Members it contained.

Hac non deteriore, &c] This Piece was on the Ground-Floor, and
contained five Parts, viz a *Cœnatio*, two *Diæta*, a *Cryptoporticus*, and
another *Diæta*, or principal Appartment; the firft of which, as well
as the two *Diæta*, being to be paffed in the Way to the *Cryptoporticus*, he therefore takes notice of, before that principal Part At fome
particular times he tells us he returned from his main Houfe to this
in the Garden, and doubtlefs carried feveral of his Family with him, for
whofe Ufe thefe two firft Appartments were defigned, and the *Cœnatio*,
as the common Eating-room for all thofe that retired with him: This
he mentions as diftant from the Sea, in comparifon of the firft-mentioned
Cœnatio It is very difficult to determine what the Profpect he fays was
enjoyed by this Room might be, though poffibly it was that of the Garden and the Seas beyond it. If we may fuppofe it to have been an Eating-
room for Summer as well as Winter, we may imagine its Windows had
a *North* Profpect of the Woods and Mountains. By the Profpects from
the Windows of the *Diæta*, and by the Difpofition of the *Cryptoporticus*, it appears that they lay *South-Eaft* of the *Cœnatio*, though, as
Winter Rooms, the Windows might have looked to other Points.
Their Profpects were different from any yet mentioned, as if he affected
to have different Views from every Appartment, or if any were repeated, it fhould be with fome Alteration, fo as to make them appear
ftill new. Thofe from thefe Rooms feem to have been of the meaneft
fort;

fort, confisting chiefly of the Kitchen-Garden and the Front of the Villa it felf, of which this *Vestibulum* was the chief Part, and placed in the Middle The *Atrium*, which must have been seen at the same time with the *Vestibulum*, being only a bare *Area*, was not so well worthy Obfervation as the Profpect of that which lay beyond it, and was joined to the Offices that were on the *South-West* side of the Houfe.

Hinc Cryptoporticus, &c] The Room he is now about to defcribe, and which was the greater Part of this Building, feems to have been an Invention fince *Vitruvius*, who makes mention of no fuch Part in his Account of the *Roman* Houfes, tho' by the following Defcription of it, and the Ufes, it appears to have been very neceffary in a Country Houfe, where the Perfon inhabiting went through fuch a daily Courfe of Exercife as our Author did The Form of it. or in what manner it was built, does not appear by his Account. But without doubt it was a long Room, and there was one manner common to all of them, which, as its Name implies, was that of a *Porticus*, enclos'd by a Wall on all fides, differing no otherwife from our prefent Galleries, than that they had Pillars in them This Room *Pliny* has here confidered under three Heads. Firft, its Size, fecondly, its Continuance to admit or exclude the Wind and Light at pleafure, and, laftly, with refpect to the Heat of the Sun both in Winter and Summer In this Place he feems to follow the Rule of Conveniency rather than that of proportioning Rooms to the main Building, as appears by the Character he gives to this of its being equal in Size to publick Buildings, and to which no other Rooms in or about this Villa bore any Equality The Reafon of this extraordinary Grandeur muft have been in confideration of the Ufe for which it was defigned, which was that of Walking : Befides, as this appears to have been a Room in which he propofed to enjoy the Pleafures of Summer as well as Winter, it muft at that Seafon, by its Capacioufnefs, have been cooler, and the Sun, by means of the Breadth of the Room, always avoided ; at the fame time one Side of it was fhady though all the Windows were open, and the Air had a thorough Paffage, as the Profpect of the Room it

self

a *Cenatio remota a Mari*

b *Diatta Dua*

c *Cryptoporticus*

d *Heliocaminus*

e *Zotheca*

f *Cubiculum noctis & somni*

g *Andron*

h *Procoton*

i *Cubiculum*

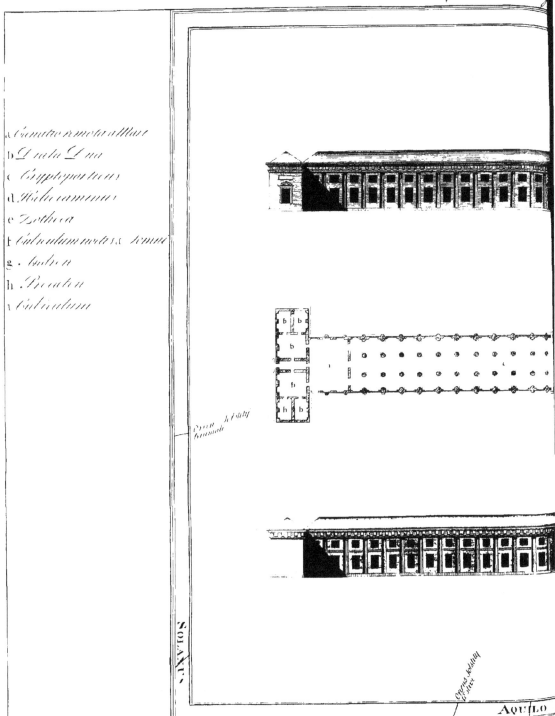

AQUILO

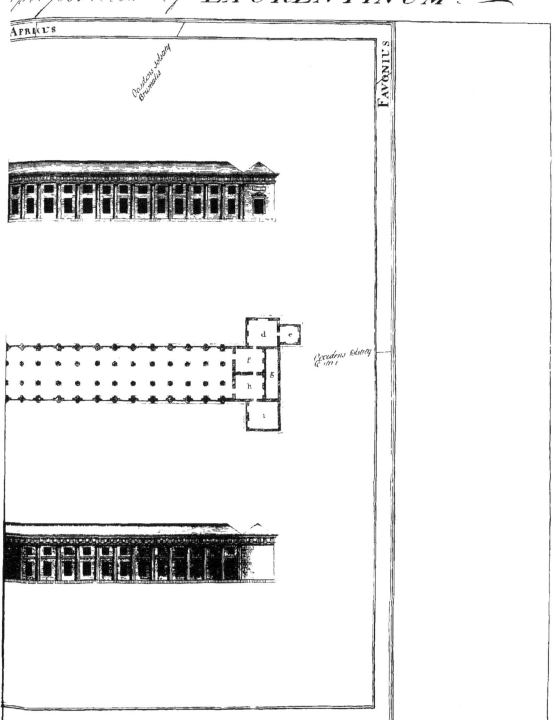

AFRICUS

FAVONIUS

Occidens solstiti Brumalis

Occidens solstiti & sun

d e

f g

h

l

felf was more agreeable to those that walked in it. The Method taken in this Room to receive the Benefit, and avoid the Inconveniences, of the Wind at all times, was nothing more than two Ranges of Windows on each fide; and though this Room had Conveniences for Summer, yet, as if he was defirous to have more for Winter, those that were on the *South-Weft* fide were large, and two Ranges compleat, and those on the *North-Eaft* were lefs, with the upper Range not equal in Number to thofe of the lower. The principal Convenience of thofe Windows on both fides, he tells us himfelf, was, that as Occafion required, thofe Winds that were agreeable might be admitted, and the others excluded. Befides the Advantage of Air in *lib* 1 *cp* 21 he alfo tells us a particular one that thefe two Ranges of Windows were of to him who was afflicted with bad Eyes. His Words are, *Cryptoporticus quoque adopertis inferioribus fineftris tantum Umbræ quantum Luminis habet.*

Ante Cryptoporticus Xyflus, &c.] Hitherto he has only mentioned the Advantages this Room had within it felf; but here he comes to confider of what Benefit it was to whatever lay neareft it (as did the *Xyflus* on the *South-Weft*) in the fame manner as when he is fpeaking of that of *Tufcum, lib* 9 *cp* 36 he fays, as the Weather directed he either walked in that or the *Cryptoporticus* about the fourth or fifth Hour of the Day, at which time the Sun fhining directly on that fide of the *Cryptoporticus*, its Heat was encreafed in the *Xyflus* by the Oppofition it met from the *Cryptoporticus*, which, on that Account made it more agreeable during the Winter, and was equally advantageous to it during the fame Seafon, by keeping off the *North-Eaft* Winds, and oppofing a thorough Paffage on the *South-Weft*.

Hæc Jucunditas ejus Hyeme, major Æftate, &c.] This Pleafure proceeded rather from the Seafon, than the Difpofition of the *Cryptoporticus*; for it could not have been better placed to have made the *Xyflus* more agreeable in Winter than it really was, and the Shade and Cool-

M   nefs

n.*s* on the *North-Eaſt* ſide was only proper for Summer Beſides the *Xyſtus*, which was an open Walk both for Winter and Summer, it has been before obſerved, that there was cloſe to the *Geſtatio* another, which was covered with Vines, and ſeems to have been deſigned for walking in Summer: This being joined to the *Geſtatio* is what he here calls the neareſt Part of it, by the help of which, with the *Xyſtus* and *Cryptoporticus*, he had ſufficiently provided that no Seaſon ſhould interrupt his Exerciſe, ſince he could always walk in the Shade, and be cool during the greateſt Heats of Summer · For in the Morning before the Sun ſhone on the *South-Weſt* Side of the *Cryptoporticus*, the *Xyſtus* was ſhaded, when the Sun was advanced ſo far *Southward* as to ſhine directly on its Roof, ſo that the Building caſt no Shade, the Room it ſelf was ſhaded by its Roof; and the Windows being open at the ſame time, had a thorough Air from the Sea and the Winds that then blew; and when the Sun was got ſo far *Weſtward* as to ſhine into the *Cryptoporticus*, and make it warm, then that Building caſt a Shade on its *North-Eaſt* Side, and the Garden and neareſt Part of the *Geſtatio* became pleaſant to walk in

In Capite Xyſti, &c] At one End of the *Cryptoporticus* were two Apartments, of which Notice has been already taken, and at the other lay his own *Diæta*, in which, he ſays, he greatly delighted, and for that reaſon gave it the Name of his *Delight* or *Loves* And it appears by ſeveral Authors, to have been a thing cuſtomary in thoſe Times, to give proper Names to any principal Room or Appartment This *Diæta* ſeems to have been for his own proper Uſe, when he retired from the Manſion Houſe, which was chiefly during the *Saturnalia* in Winter ; but that it might be alſo pleaſant in Summer as well as the *Cryptoporticus*, Care was taken to adapt it to that Seaſon as well as to Study, for which reaſon this *Diæta* contained five Rooms, which was a greater Number than uſual, as appears by ſome Parts of his Deſcription He begins his Account of this *Diæta* with his two Day-chambers, the *Heliocaminus* and *Zotheca*; the former of which, by its Poſition, ſeems wholly deſigned

for

for Winter, and the other, upon all Accounts, moft proper for Summer; and doubtlefs, though not mentioned by him, both were Parts of their private Houfes in the Time of *Vitruvius* The *Heliocaminus* was extremely well guarded by the *Cryptoporticus* from all cold Winds, and as advantageoufly placed to receive the Heat of the Sun, which (as has been before obferved in the *Gymnafium*) was encreafed by the Angle made by the *Cryptoporticus* and this Room, the Windows of which he does not fo much take notice of on the Account of the Profpect, as of the Sun; for though the *Xyftus* was adorned with Flowers in the Summer, it could not have been a very beautiful Profpect in the Winter, and what he fays about the Doors and Windows having a View of the *Cryptoporticus* and *Cubiculum*, feems only with a defign to fhew the Pofition of this Room; nor was this then only Care, fince there was a particular Manner of paving thefe Rooms, which *Palladius* fpeaks of, *lib* 6 *tit* 11 And probably this Room, for the Reafon he gives, was fo paved. The *Zotheca*, or Summer or Autumn Day-chamber (in which Seafon, *lib*. 9. *cp* 36 he fays he refrefhed himfelf with Day Sleep, and which, *cp* 40. he tells us he never did in Winter) by its Pofition was fheltered from the Sun by the *Heliocaminus*, till the Hour of Sleep was over, and the Sun was paffed more *Weftward*; before which Time, by reafon of the Openings on all Sides of this Room, it muft have been very cool by Breezes from the Sea, and by the Aperture on one fide to the *North-Eaft* The Account of the Furniture of this Room, though it fhews its Ufe, feems introduced for no other reafon than to denote its Size. For fpeaking of the *Zothecula* of *Tufcum*, he mentions lefs Furniture than in this larger *Zotheca* From this Room (having Windows on three fides, and Jettings-out *Weftward* beyond any other Building near this Part) there was an Opportunity, though on the Ground-floor, of feeing three Profpects, which he efteemed the moft agreeable about his Houfe, *viz* the *North-Eaft* Profpect of the Woods (which he alfo fays could be feen from the principal *Triclinium*) that of the Sea which lay to the *South-Weft*, and, laftly, that of the neighbouring Villas, with which that Shore was covered. The Account he gives of feeing thefe

Profpects

Prospects *à pedibus*, &c must be spoken with relation to the Position of the Bed, which could not have been any where so commodiously placed in such a small Room with Windows on all sides, as in the Middle, by which means it had the Benefit of more Air, and it must have been from the Middle of the Room that he could see all the fore-mentioned Prospects separate and distinct, which, upon a nearer Approach to any Window, must have appeared intermingled.

Junctum est Cubiculum Noctis & Somni, &c] From the Description of the Day-chambers he proceeds to that which he distinguishes from them by telling us its Office. This was the Room into which the Folding-doors of the *Heliocaminus* opened, and its principal Qualifications were, that it was free from Noise and Light; and the Method he employed to accomplish these Ends he himself accounts for. The Noises he seems so careful to avoid, were those common to all Villas seated near the Sea, as well as that of the young Slaves, who, at the time this *Duet* was most in use, had the Liberty of doing almost what they pleased. He was so far from suffering the Glare of Lightning to enter the Room, that he took care to have it in his Power to keep out even the Light of the Day, as long as he thought proper, for the Reasons he gives, *l.b 9. ep 36 clausa Fenestra manent, mirè enim Silentio & Tenebris Animus alitur*

Applicitum est Cubiculo Hypocaustum, &c] Though Noise and Light were excluded this Room, it had still wanted one great Conveniency if there had not been an *Hypocaustum* to heat it in Winter Nights, and it may be observed, that in no other Room of this Winter Villa he mentions any Care taken for that purpose, except in his two Night-Chambers, as if he either chose to warm himself by Exercise, or retiring to those Rooms that were warm by their Position, as most of his for the Day were, than by the Heat of a Fire, which was only used to give a moderate Warmth to his Bed-chamber in cold Nights; and by the Account he gives of this *Hypocaustum*, it seems very much to resemble that of the other *Dormitorium*. The Methods taken to prevent

the

the Noife and Light, muft have been an Advantage to this Room in Summer, by keeping off the Sun all the Day, and making it alfo a proper Bed-chamber for that Seafon

Procœton] It appears by what he fays, *lib* 9 *ep* 36 that it was his Cuftom every Morning to have his *Notarius* attend to write down what he fhould dictate, and not improbably this Room was his Bed-chamber, as it was joined to that of the Mafter, and by its Defcription feems that of a Servant Neither in this Place, or in any other Part of this Villa, where he mentions fuch Rooms, does he take notice of any Benefit they had either of Sun, Air, or Profpect, and we may therefore conclude this Room, as well as the Night-chamber, looked into the *Andron*

Cubiculum porrigitur in Solem, &c] This *Cubiculum*, by its Defcription, feems to have been a Room for Books and Study, one of which he had alfo in his *Diæta* in the main Houfe, though this, by its Defcription, was placed much more commodious for that Ufe, and, according to the Rules laid down by *Vitruvius, lib* 6 *cap* 7 was fheltered from the *South* and *Weft* Winds by other Buildings, and turned fo as to have the Benefit of the Morning Sun The Reafon of their thus difpofing their Libraries, *Vitruvius* in the fame Chapter tells us, was becaufe the Morning was the Time in which thofe Rooms were moftly ufed, and their being opened to the *Eaft* preferved the Books from the Mold and Rottennefs that a *South* or *Weft* Difpofition would have caufed

Hæc Amœnitas, &c] With the *Bibliotheca* ends the Defcription of what he calls *Gratiam Villæ*, and here he enters upon the Situation, which he confiders under two Heads, *viz Opportunitatem Loci, & Litoris Spatium*; the latter of which only regards the Pleafure of the Place, but under the other is confidered every Article neceffary to be obferved in all Situations, *viz*. Health, Air, Provifions, Roads, and good Water : As to the Air of this Place, as has been before obferved,

N   it

it was needlefs here to fpeak of it, and the Roads from *Rome* he has
fufficiently fpoke of at the Beginning of his Epiftle; and as he was
feated clofe to the Sea, and not far from *Oftia*, there was no Occafion
to take notice of the Conveniency of water Carriage· There remained
then only to account for what we may call the Goodnefs of the Water
and Provifions· In his Obfervations on the firft of which he is more particular, becaufe, in whatever Degree that Element was good or bad, it
was Matter of Confequence to the Health as well as Conveniency of
the Inhabitant, and he therefore here takes notice of what feldom hap-
pens in Ground clofe to, and almoft upon a level with, the Sea, that
the Water was not any ways brackifh The only Inconveniency of this
Water was, that, lying fo low, it could not, without Labour or En-
gines, be brought to ferve the Bath, and all other Offices of the Houfe;
for he could not mean it as a Defect in this Winter Villa, to have wanted
Fountains, more efpecially as it lay near the Sea, which was fo vifible
from all its Parts, that even in Summer it would rather have been a
Pleafure to have been free from the Sight of fuch a Profufion of Water
in the retired Parts of the Garden, if there were any, for thofe that are
defcribed feem to have been all within Sight of the Sea

It is neceffary, in this Place, to obferve what *Pliny* fays concerning
this Villa, *lib 4 ep 6 Nihil quidem ibi poffideo præter Tectum & Hortum, ftatimque Arenas*; fince upon this Account it is that he here takes
no notice of the Fruitfulnefs of the Soil, and other Advantages proper
to be confidered in fuch a Villa as *Tufcum*, being here obliged (though
in the Country) to buy all manner of Provifion, which is what *Martial*
ridicules, *lib 3 epig 36* and *Varro, lib 3 cap 1.* will not allow that
a Country Houfe, no otherwife fupplied, deferves the Name of a Villa:
However, thofe that built on choice Spots of Ground fo near *Rome,* were
generally reduced to the fame Neceffity with *Pliny*

Suggerunt affatim Ligna proxima Sylva] The Conveniency of Life
which he next confiders, is that of Fuel, with which he was fufficiently
furnifhed

furnifhed from thofe very Woods which created fo beautiful a Profpect in feveral Parts of the Villa.

Cæteras Copias, &c] Since he was obliged to buy all his Provifions, it was no fmall Conveniency to have been in the Neighbourhood of fuch a Town as *Oftia,* from whence even *Rome* it felf was furnifhed with all fuch as were thought worth importing from foreign Parts ; and common Neceffaries, he tells us, could be had from that Village that probably gave Name to this Villa.

In hoc Balinea, &c] Bathing, in his Time, was become fo habitual, that it is here reckoned among the Neceffaries of Life.

Litus ornant Varietate gratiffima, &c] Our Author, in this Place, comes to fpeak of *Litoris Spatium,* which was the third Head he propofed to confider, and here fhews that he meant no more by it, than the extenfive Profpect of the neighbouring Sea-coaft   The pleafant Shore of the *Tyrrhene* Sea had induced many of the principal *Romans* thereon to erect their Villas , but the Part of it on which they were moft numerous, was that near *Baia,* and round the Gulf of *Naples,* where, as *Pliny* tells us, *lib. 9 ep* 7. they built them on two different Situations, *viz* one on the Top of the Rocks, to command a larger Profpect of the Sea, as was that famous one of *Lucullus* near *Mifenum* , and the other as this of *Pliny,* clofe to, and almoft level with the Water, the more immediately to enjoy the Pleafures of the Sea it felf: The former, by its lofty Situation, he compares to the Tragedian raifed on his *Cothurni*; and the humble Lownefs of the other, to the Comedian in his *Socculi* ; and though he had the Pleafure of both thefe Situations in his two Villas on the Lake of *Comum,* and could, as Occafion required, remove from one to the other, yet here on the Sea, where we do not find he had more than one, he prefers the lower Site, having, as his Defcription fhews, fufficiently guarded againft all Inconveniences that could arife from its lying fo low. The Situation preventing his taking in the whole Shore,

and

and all its Beauties, at one View, from any one Part of the Villa, he chooses here to describe the Prospects as seen by those that were either at Sea, or on the Sands, where they had a distinct View of the Villas that were seated near the Sea, which, by the Mixture of Trees with the Houses, as he observes, must have been more agreeable than a continued View of Buildings, as in Cities.

Quod nonnunquam, &c] Having described the Beauties of the Coast, he very properly introduces the Conveniency and Pleasure of its Sands for Travelling, and in what sort of Fish the Sea abounded.

Villa vero nostra, &c.] In this Passage he prepares to obviate the Objections that might possibly be raised to such a Situation as this, which, though it might have Plenty of Fish proper to it, must yet have wanted the Necessaries to be found in an Inland Situation. These he here answers.

Villula nostra] Though he gives to this House the Name of a small Villa, it appears, that after having described but Part of it, yet, if every *Diæta* may be supposed to contain three Rooms, he has taken notice of no less than forty-six, besides all which there remains near half the House undescribed, which was, as he says, allotted to the Use of the Servants; and it is very probable this Part was made uniform with that he has already described. As he here had no Ground for Pasturage or Tillage, doubtless there were no Rooms set apart for hind Servants, or any thing belonging to Agriculture; so that these Offices only contained proper Rooms for dressing the Meals and Entertainments, and some in which they were preparatorily stored with several others for several different Uses, for the Disposition of all which there are Rules given by those Authors he has followed in the Disposition of the *Prætorium.* The *Culina, Columella, lib* 1 *cap* 6 directs to be large and lofty, the better to avoid danger from Fire, and to contain their Servants (as we may guess, at their Meals) and *Vitruvius* advises it to be

placed

placed in some warm Part of the House. This Room, being the Chief of the Offices, is in the Plan, placed to answer the *Cella Frigidaria*, consisting of as large a Size. As it was guarded by Buildings from all cold Winds, and looked into the *Cavædium*, and the Openings turned to the *Weſt* and *South*, it anſwers the Diſpoſition *Vitruvius* directs. Betwixt this Room and the *Dormitorium* are three Cells, for the *Notarius* and two other Freedmen, on the other ſide joining to the *Focus* are the *Cortinale*, or Room in which they boiled their New Wine, mentioned by *Columella*, *lib* 1 *cap.* 9 and the *Furnus*, with deſign that all thoſe Parts that required Fire, might be in one Place ſupplyed. Beyond theſe Rooms is the *Carnarium*; and the *Ergaſtulum*, where they kept their Slaves at Work, and which *Columella*, *lib* 1 *cap.* 6. directs to be made under Ground, the better to ſecure them, is in this Villa otherwiſe diſpoſed. Since in ſuch a low watery Soil his Rule could not well be kept, it is therefore here upon a level with the other Buildings, and being by its Office obliged to be very capacious, is placed ſo as to anſwer the largeſt Room on the other ſide, which was the *Sphæriſterium*. To anſwer the two *Turres*, that are deſcribed on the other ſide of the Houſe, in the Plan are two more erected for Offices, in the more *Eaſtern* are the *Cella Vinaria*, being turned *Northerly*, and the *Olearia* to the *South*, as *Vitruvius* directs, *lib* 6 *cap* 9 The two lower Floors of the Building that are adequate to this, contain but one huge *Triclinium*; but here they are divided, and over the Cells for Wine and Oil are Servants Rooms, as are alſo in both the Floors of the other *Turris*; but on the Top of this is placed the *Oporotheca*, or Room to preſerve Fruit, mentioned by *Varro*, *lib* 1 *cap.* 62 where he orders the Windows to be placed as theſe are. The Diſpoſition of that Building which anſwers the *Piſcina* of the Baths, the beſt correſponds to that which *Columella*, *lib* 1 *cap* 6 directs for the Cells of the Freedmen. The *Equilia* are placed at a ſmall Diſtance from the Houſe, and turned to a warm Quar-

O

ter,

ter, according to *Vitruvius*, and *Palladius*, *lib* 1 *tit* 30. would have the *Lignarium* and *Fœnile* to be, as these in the Plan, distant from the Villa, for fear of Fire; and in *tit* 31. the last-mentioned Author says there ought to be two *Piscina*, one for the Use of the Cattle, and the other for those of the House: This Rule we may therefore conclude, was certainly observed in the *Villa Urbana*, as well as the *Villa Rustica*.

The

THE

VILLAS of the ANCIENTS

ILLUSTRATED.

PART II

SINCE it has been obferved in the former Part of this Work, that *Varro* denies fuch an Houfe as has been defcrib'd by *Pliny* to deferve the Name of a *Villa*, it may not be improper to examine what it was that this and other Authors on Agriculture efteem'd neceffary to a compleat *Villa*, and was confider'd and practifed by the Architect, when neither the Nature of the Place nor Circumftances of the Mafter did forbid, all which may be reduced under the three following Heads, viz the Situation, the *Villa*, and what the *French* call the Environs of the *Villa*

The Choice of a Situation with refpect to the Soil, whether proper to bear Corn, Wine, and Oil, feems to have been rather the Province of the Husbandman But if the Architect had Liberty to chufe where to build, it were juftly to be expected that the Situation fhould be both healthy and convenient *Columella, lib* 1 *cap* 2 gives the Defcription of a moft eligible Situation in the following Words *If Fortune would favour me in my Defire, I could wifh to have an Eftate in a wholefome Climate and fruitful Country, one Part champian, another Hilly with*

P

eafy

caſy Deſcents either to the Eaſt or South, ſome of the Lands cultivated, others wild and woody, not far from the Sea or a navigable River, for the eaſier Exportation of the Produce of the Farm and the Importation of Neceſſaries The Champain lying below the Houſe ſhould be diſpos'd into Grounds for Paſture and Tillage, Oſiers and Reeds, ſome of the Hills ſhould be naked and without Trees that they may ſerve only for Corn which grows in a Soil moderately dry and rich, better than in ſteep Grounds Wherefore the upper Corn Fields ſhould have as little Declivity as poſſible, and ought to reſemble as it were the Plain, from thence the other Hills ſhould be laid out into Olive Grounds and Vineyards, and produce Trees neceſſary to make Props for thoſe Fruits, and if Occaſion ſhould require Building, to afford Timber and Stone, and alſo Paſture for Cattle Moreover conſtant Rivulets of Water ſhould deſcend from thence upon the Meadows, Gardens and Oſier Grounds, and alſo ſerve for the Conveniency of the Cattle that graze in the Fields and Thickets But ſuch a Situation is not eaſily to be met with, that which enjoys moſt of theſe Advantages is certainly moſt valuable, that which has them in a moderate Degree is not deſpicable The natural good Qualities of a Situation mention'd by *Palladius, lib 1 cap 2* are a ſalutary Air, plenty of wholeſome Water, a fruitful Soil, and a commodious Place, and in the two following Chapters he thus directs how to judge of the Goodneſs of Air and Water *We may conclude thoſe Places wholeſome that are not in deep Vallies, nor ſubject to thick Clouds, where the Inhabitants are of a freſh Complexion, clear Head, good Sight, quick Hearing, and a free diſtinct Speech By theſe Means is the goodneſs of the Air diſtinguiſh'd, but the contrary Appearance proclaims that Climate to be noxious. The unwholeſomeneſs of Water may be thus diſcover'd In the firſt Place it muſt not be convey'd from Ditches or Fens, nor riſe from Minerals, but be very tranſparent, not tainted either in Taſte or Smell, without Settlement, in Winter warm, in Summer cold But becauſe Nature often conceals a more fatal Miſchief in theſe outward Appearances, we may judge whether Water is good by the Health of the Inhabitants, if their Cheeks are clean, their Heads ſound, and little or no Decay in their Lungs and Breaſts For generally when the Diſtempers in the upper Part of the Body are tranſmitted down to the lower, as from the Head to the Lungs or Stomach, then the Air is infectious Beſides if the Belly, Bowels, Sides,*

or

or Reins are not afflicted with Aches or Tumours, and there is no Ulcer in the Bladder; if these or the like are apparently in the major Part of the Inhabitants, there is no Cause to suspect the Unwholsomenefs of the Air or Water. The fatal Consequences proceeding from a bad Air, *Varro* tells us, *lib* 1 *cap* 5 are in some Meafure to be alleviated, if not prevented, by the Skill of the Architect His Words are thefe *That Land which is most wholfome is most profitable, because there is a certain Crop Whereas on the contrary in an unhealthy Country, notwithstanding the Ground is fertile, yet Sickness will not allow the Husbandman to reap the Fruits of his Labour For where one exposes his Life to certain Dangers for uncertain Advantages, not only the Crop, but the Life of the Inhabitant is precarious Wherefore if it is not wholfome, the Tillage is nothing elfe but the Hazard of the Owner's Life and his Family; but this Inconveniency is remedied by Knowledge, for Health, which proceeds from the Air and Soil, is not in our Dispofal, but under the Guidance of Nature, yet neverthelefs it is much in our Power to make that Burthen eafy by our own Care, which is heavy by Nature For if upon the Account of the Land or Water, or some unfavory fmell which makes an Irruption in some Part of it, the Farm is more unwholfome, or upon Account of the Climate, or a bad Wind that blows, the Ground is heated, these Inconveniencies may be remedied by the Skill and Expence of the Owner which makes it of the last Concernment where the Villas are placed, how large they are, and to what Quarters then Porticus, Gates and Windows are turn'd. Did not* Hippocrates *the Physician, in the Time of a great Plague, preserve not only his own Farm, but many Towns by his Skille But why do I call him in as a Witness? Did not* Varro, *when his Army and Fleet lay at* Corcyra, *and every House was fill'd with fick Persons and dead Bodies, by his Care in making new Windows to the North Laft, and obftructing the Infection by altering the Position of the Doors, and things of the like Nature, preserve his Companions and Family in good Health* Thefe Confiderations seem to have govern'd the same Author in the Rules he gives for placing the Villa in *lib* 1 *cap* 13 and alfo *Columella* in thofe he has fo fully deliver'd on the same Subject, *lib* 1 *cap* 4, & 5 which latter, as they may be of fingular Service, I shall deliver entire and are as follow *As an House should be built in a wholfome Country, fo it should in the most whole-*

fome

some Part of the Country For *an open Air, and at the same Time infected, causes many Distempers* Some *Places are not hot in the Summer Solstice, but suffer much from the Severity of the Winter, as it is reported of* Thebes *in Bœotia* Others, *like* Chalcis *in* Eubœa, *are warm in Winter and excessive hot in the Summer* An Air *temperate both as to Heat and Cold is to be chosen, like that on an Hill moderately high, because by not being too low it does not suffer through Frosts in Winter, nor is it scorch'd by the Vapours in Summer, and the Top of an Hill is to be avoided, that being afflicted with too sharp Winds or constant Rains* Therefore *the Situation in the Middle of an Hill is best, the Ground on which the House stands swelling in some Measure, to hinder the Foundation from being riven or torn by an impetuous Torrent rushing from the Top* There *should be a constant Spring either within the Villa itself or brought from without, with Timber and Pasture adjacent* If there *is no running Stream, some Well Water must be found out in the Neighbourhood, not deep, nor of a bitter or brackish Taste* Should *these Conveniencies likewise fail, and there is great Scarcity of running Water, large Cisterns must be made for Men, and Ponds for Cattle, to hold the Rain Water, which is most wholesome, but that is esteem'd best which is convey'd by earthen Pipes into a cover'd Cistern* Next *to this is the running Water that takes its Rise from the Mountains, if in its Fall it passes through Rocks, as in* Garcenum *in* Campania *The third in order of Goodness is the Well Water or that which springs out of an Hill, or is not found in a very deep Vail* The worst *Sort is that in the Fen which runs but slowly, that is infectious which stagnates there* This Water *is of a pernicious Quality, yet in the Winter by the Rains the Malignity abates which is the Reason that Rain Water is generally esteem'd wholesome, because it washes off the Noisomeness of the poisonous Water* But *we have already said this is not approved of for drinking* Running *Streams however chiefly conduce to our Refreshment in hot Weather, and to render the Place delightful, which as long as they continue sweet, if the Nature of the Place will admit of it, in my Opinion ought to be convey'd into the* Villa But *if a River should be remote from Hills, and the Healthfulness of the Place and the Situation of an high Bank should permit you to build your* Villa *above the River, Care must be taken that the River runs rather behind than before the House, and that the Front of the Villa may be turn'd from the hurtful Winds of that Country, and face the most*
                                                            Healthful,

Healthful, Rivers generally being infested with sultry Vapours in Summer and cold Fogs in Winter, which are pernicious to Man and Beast, unless dissipated by the greater Force of Winds. The most Advantageous Situation in wholesome Places is, as I said before, when turn'd to the East or South, in a foggy Air to the North. The Sea is always directly to be turn'd to, yet not so as to have the House dash'd and sprinkled by its Waves, or but just removed from the Strand, for it is better to be situated at some considerable Distance from the Sea, because the intermediate Space has a thicker Air. Neither should Villas join to a Marsh or a high Road, because in hot Weather the one ejects its poisonous Quality and breeds Insects armed with Stings, which invade us in full Swarms. Besides it emits the Infection of Water Snakes and Serpents that is left in the Winter's Filth and Mud and envenom'd with fomented Nastiness, from whence proceed many secret Distempers for which the Physicians themselves cannot account. And also the whole Year round the Situation and Water spoil the Utensils of Husbandry, and all the Houshold Furniture, at the same Time rotting the standing as well as gather'd Fruits. The other is inconvenient upon account of frequent Passengers pillaging, and the constant Entertainment of Sportsmen. Wherefore, to avoid all these Inconveniences, I think it proper to build a Villa neither on the Road nor in an infectious Place, but at a good Distance off, and upon a rising Ground, that it may front exactly the Equinoctial Sun rising, for such a Situation preserves an equal Temperament between Winter and Summer Winds, and by how much the more towards the East the House stands, by so much the more freely may it receive the Air in Summer, be exempted from the Storms of Winter, and refreshed by the Morning Sun, which thaws the frozen Dews. It being reckon'd almost Pestilential if the Situation be remote from the Sun and warm Breezes, which if it does not enjoy, no other Power can dry up the nocturnal Dews, and purify the other Mildews and Blasts which may settle upon the Corn, those Things which are infectious to Men being undoubtedly prejudicial to Cattle, Vegetables, and Fruits.

The foregoing Rules having directed the Architect in the Choice of a proper Situation, and in the most advantageous Placing the House, the next Thing to be consider'd was the *Villa* itself, in which the Size, Disposition, Number and Quality of the several Members were carefully observed.

Q

The

The *Villa*, Columella *(lib 1 cap 6)* tells us, was divided into three Parts, *viz* The *Urbana* or the Master's Part, the *Rustica* or that Part allotted to the Use of the Husbandmen, Cattle, and the proper Offices of the Farm The *third* Part was called *Fructuaria*, because it consisted of Store Houses for Corn, Wine, Oyl, and other Fruits of the Earth The Size of the first and Number of Parts it contain'd were determin'd by the Pleasure or Quality of the Master, but those Parts belonging to Agriculture, by the Bulk of the Farm and Number of the Cattle The Servants that in most great Mens Houses were more immediately for the Master's Use, and may be said to belong to the *Villa Urbana*, were the *Atrienses*, which included all what we call Livery Servants and those belonging to the Bed-Chamber, the *Topiarii*, which were Gardeners belonging to the Pleasure Garden, Comedians, Musicians, and the *Notarius* or Secretary The principal Person over the other Parts of the *Villa* was the *Procurator* or Bailif, then the *Villicus* or Husbandman, who had under his Care the Tillage of the Land, and the Disposal of the Produce of the Earth about the *Villa*, next was the *Villica* or House keeper, to whose Care every Thing within Doors belong'd, and had immediately under her Command the Women Servants that were employ'd on those Affairs, but particularly those belonging to the feeding and cloathing of the Houshold The Master of the Cattle may take the next Place, and under his Command were all the Herdsmen, Shepherds, Goatherds, Swincherds, and Grooms The Care of all those Fowl that were within the Bounds of the *Villa* was committed to the *Aviarius*, which may not improperly be call'd the Poulterer In great *Villas* that were far from a Town, it was thought proper to keep within the Family several Sorts of useful Mechanicks, as Smiths, Carpenters, &c all which were under the Inspection of the Master of the Works The Slaves were under the Care of the *Ergastularius*, a Person so call'd from the Name of the Lodging or Working-House in which those unhappy Wretches were confin'd

The Cattle within the *Villa* were Horses and Mules, which seem to have been retain'd for the Master's Use, being never employ'd about the Tillage of the Farm, which were wholly perform'd by Asses and

Oxen,

Oxen, befides which, Provifion was made for all other Sorts of Cattle The Fowls within the Walls of the *Villa* were Poultrey, Pidgeons, Turtles, and the *Turdus*, which it is hard to determine pofitively what it was, only thus much we can learn from *Varro*, that it was a Bird of Paffage, and was confin'd only with them in certain Seafons

To make Provifion for lodging all thefe feveral Perfons and Animals, and alfo Places for Corn and the neceffary Offices of the Houfe, was the Architect's Care, and in the Difpofition of each Part was govern'd by Rules that may be collected from *Cato, Vitruvius, Varro, Columella,* and *Palladius* The Mafter's Part call'd by *Vitruvius, Pfeudo-Urbana,* by others *Villa Urbana,* and by fome the *Prætorium,* to give it the better Grace, was commonly placed fomething higher than the reft, it confifted of Apartments for the Mafter and his Friends, eating Rooms for different Seafons, and other Members and Ornaments of Buildings, fuitable to the Quality of the Perfon for whom it was built *Vitruvius, lib 6 cap* 8 fays, that before it was commonly a *Periftyle* or Court, furrounded with a *Porticus,* at the End of which was the *Atrium* or Hall, which had a *Porticus* alfo on each Side that look'd towards the Walks and *Palæftra,* or thofe Parts of the Garden fet afide for Bowling or the like Exercife, and may not improbably be the fame that *Palladius* calls *Pratum,* and orders to furround the *Prætorium,* fince that Word feems to have been ufed as a common Name for all Ground cover'd with Grafs In the Difpofition of the Rooms in this principal Part, Care was taken that thofe defign'd for Ufe in Winter fhould enjoy the whole Courfe of the Sun at that Seafon, and thofe for the Summer to avoid the Heats of that Seafon as much as poffible The Baths, which were moft commonly joining to the *Prætorium,* were (as has been before obferved) always turn'd fo as to enjoy the Winter's fetting Sun

Over the Gateway or Entrance of the other Part of the *Villa,* the Procurator had his Lodging, and Rooms for other Conveniences, on one Side of the Gate (efpecially if there was no Porter) was lodged the *Villicus,* and had Store Rooms near him where he kept all the Utenfils of Husbandry, and deliver'd them out as Occafion requir'd The *Villica* having under her Care thofe Rooms where Stores of Provifion vision were kept, it was necessary she should not be lodged far from her Charge, which Rule was likewise observed in disposing of all the other principal Servants. The other Freemen that were Servants had Lodging Rooms turned to the South, and the Slaves were lodged in one common Room call'd *Ergastulum*, by *Columella, lib* 1 *cap* 6 made under Ground, the better to prevent their making their Escape. And the *Valetudinarium* or Infirmary, mention'd by the same Author *lib* 12 *cap* 3 was doubtless so placed as not to annoy any Part of the *Villa*, nor so as that the Persons there lodged should be any Ways incommoded by the rest of the Family.

The Room that is mention'd as the principal Member of every *Villa Rustica*, was the Kitchen, in which was the only Fire Place or Chimney in that Part, and in the account of some *Villas*, there is mention made of no other Room for the Servants to eat in, tho' indeed *Varro* speaks of another which may be call'd the Servants Hall. Next to the Kitchen the principal Rooms were the Repositories for Oyl and new Wines, for there was also an *Apotheca* or Cellar for old Wines, in some of their *Villas* placed not far from the Kitchen, so as to have the Benefit of the Smoak, which hastens Wine to a Maturity, and near the same Kitchen, so as to partake of the Chimney, was the Room call'd *Cortinale*, where the new Wines were boil'd. The Room where the Wines were press'd and kept while new, had its Windows opening to the North, and where the Oyls were press'd and kept, to the South Dependent on the Kitchen, and not far remov'd from it were the Larders, and House-keeper's Store Rooms, and the Spinning Rooms may be thought not to be improperly placed near the Lodging of the *Villica*. The Granaries receiv'd their Light mostly from the North or North East, and for the Sake of keeping the Corn free from Moisture, they were commonly boarded and placed over some other Rooms. The *Oporotheca*, where several Sorts of Fruits were preserved, was also turn'd the same Way, and to keep the Fruit still more cool, these Repositories were sometimes pav'd and lin'd with Marble, at least as high as the Fruit came. The Stalls for Oxen, by the particular Direction of *Vitruvius* and *Palladius*, were adjoin'd to the Kitchen so as to have a View of the Fire, which it seems those Creatures delight

light in, and it caufes them to have a fmoother Coat. *Cato* gives Directions for two Sorts of Stalls, *viz.* One for Summer call'd *Falifca* opening to the North, and the other call'd *Profepe* for Winter, and turn'd to the South. The Stalls for Cows requir'd the fame Care, but it was not thought neceffary that they fhould be placed fo near the Kitchen as the other. The Stables for Horfes were turn'd to the South, but not to have a View of the Fire as the Oxen had, it having a different effect upon them. The Goats and Sheep had Quarters allotted to them within the *Villa*, at leaft for fome of the more tender Sort, as the *Tarentine* and the *Afiatic*, and the other Cattle were lodged either in or near the Houfe. Both *Vitruvius* and *Palladius* agree, that the *Villa Ruftica* was furrounded by a Court or Farm-yard, and mention only one, but *Varro* mentions two, one of which he calls the Inner-Court, and anfwers the Defcription of the *Cavaedium difpluviatum* mention'd by *Vitruvius*, *lib* 6 *cap* 3 and the Rain Water that ran from the Roofs of the Houfe was received in a Pond in the Middle of the Court which ferved to water the Cattle, and the feveral Ufes of the Family. The Farm-yard which furrounded the Houfe was always litter'd with Straw, for the Sake of the Cattle's treading or lying foft, and had two Dunghills and a Pond in it for the foaking of Willows or the like Ufes. And if there was no Inner-Court, had alfo a Pond for the Cattle to drink at. As for thofe Parts of the *Villa* that furrounded the Inner Court, fufficient has been already fpoken. I come now to fpeak of thofe about the Farm yard, to the Wall of which that faceth the South, *Palladius* directs a *Porticus* to be made for the Cattle to retire to, to avoid the Rains and Cold in Winter, and the Heats in Summer, by the Walls of this Court were alfo built the Cart Houfes and Places to lay up the Plows and other Implements of Agriculture, that might be damaged by the Weather. The Hogftyes, that they might not annoy the Family, were likewife built under the forefaid *Porticus*, and the danger of Fire directed moft of the Builders to place the Bake houfe, and repofitories of Wood, Reeds, Straw, Hay and Leaves, diftant from the Houfe where the Family was Lodged. The Mill, when there was plenty of Water near the *Villa*, was fo placed as to be worked by the Stream, but if that

R   Conve-

Conveniency was wanting, it was still placed distant from the House. The *Area* or thrashing Floor, and the Barn call'd *Nubilarium* which adjoin'd to it, were oblig'd to be placed fartheft from the House, and for the Sake of a free Air on an open rising Ground not surrounded by any Thing, and then the Chaff which the Wind carried away was not hurtful to the Orchards and Gardens that were never the *Villa.* Without the Wall of the Farm-yard was another smaller Yard call'd *Avianum,* which was wholly fet apart for the feeding and bringing up those Fowls call'd *Aves cohortiles,* or Fowls of the Yard, to diftinguifh them from those that were bred at a further Diftance from the *Villa.* Thefe Fowls are by *Columella* faid to be of four Sorts, *viz.* the *Gallus Cohortalis* or Poultry, the Pidgeon, Turtle and *Turdus,* and becaufe the fame Author is very particular in defcribing the feveral Conveniences that were made for thefe kind of Fowl, it may not be thought improper here to give fome Account of his Directions for making them, in order to which I fhall firft begin with the *Gallinarium* or Hen houfe, *lib* 8 *cap* 3 *Hen Houfes fhould be built in that Part of the Villa that looks to the Winter's rifing Sun, contiguous to the Oven or Kitchen, that the Fowls may partake of the Smoke, which is efteem'd wholefome for this kind. In the whole Houfe there muft be three contiguous Cells, whofe whole Front muft, as I faid before, directly face the Eaft. Then in the Front let there be one fmall Paffage to the middle Cell which ought to be the leaft of the three in height, and feven Feet fquare, in which the Paffage muft be carried from the right and left Hand Wall to each Cell. Adjoining to that Wall that is oppofite to the Entrance is to be added a Chimney, fo long as not to hinder the abovemention'd Paffages, nor each Cell from partaking of the Smoke, in length and height let them be twelve Feet, then breadth not more than half their height, let them be divided by Floors, which fhall have four full Feet above and feven below, becaufe thofe Floors hold all the Fowls, each Floor ought to be appropriated to the Service of the Poultry, and enlighten'd by little Windows facing the Eaft.* In the Chapter immediately following, the fame Author fays, that *Pidgeons ought to be fed within an Houfe which fhould not be built in a cold or cold Place, but upon a rifing Ground to look to the Winter Mid-day. The Walls fill'd with continued Nefts, or if this cannot be done, let Boards be put upon Pofts driven into the Ground to receive*
                                                                      the

the Lockers or earthen Pidgeon-holes in which the Pidgeons build, Perches being placed before them through which they may pass to their Nests But the whole Place and any Cells ought to be smooth'd over with white Plaister, because Pidgeons take a particular Delight in that Colour The Walls also without should be polish'd about the Windows, which should be so disposed as to receive the Sun the greatest Part of the Winter's Day, and have a Hole large enough near it cover'd with Nets, to exclude the Hawks and receive the Pidgeons that go out to sun themselves The Rules which *Columella* gives for bringing up Turtle Doves differ little from those for the Pidgeons, only that instead of having Holes for them to build their Nests in, they had Brackets jutting out from the Walls, and were by Nets debarr'd the Liberty of flying abroad to prevent their growing lean As for the Conveniences that were thought proper to be made for the confining and fattening the Turdi or Misle-thrushes (as some think them to be) since *Varro* is most particular in his Description of those Houses, I shall here deliver what he says, *lib* 3 *cap* 4 The Roof like a Periftyle cover'd with Tyles or Nets should be large enough to contain some Thousands of Thrushes and Black Birds Some also, besides these Birds, add Linnets and Quails, because when fatten'd they bear a good Price Water ought to be convey'd by a Pipe into such an House through narrow Troughs that may easily be cleans'd The Doors should be low and narrow, and of that Sort which is call'd Cochlea, as generally those are in the Place where Bulls fight The Windows should be few, that they might not see Trees or Birds abroad, because the sight of them and the longing after them, makes the Birds that are shut up to pine away, they should have no more Light than to see where to perch and where their Meat and Drink is These Houses should be plaister'd round the Doors and Windows to prevent the Mice and other Vermin from coming in Opposite to this Aviary is another that is less, in which the dead Birds are kept, that the Overseer may give an Account to his Master When there is Occasion to have some that are fat out of the Aviary, they are shut into the less, which is call'd the Seclusorium, and is join'd to the greater by a Door and larger Light.

Every Thing within the Walls of the Farm-yard was secured from Robbers by a Guard of Porters and Dogs, who were lodged near the first Gate

Had

Had not *Varro* in *lib. 4. de Lingua Latina*, inform'd us, that the military Word *Cohors* was originally a Word belonging to a *Villa*, I might have Reason to think by the frequent Use made of that and *Prætorium* in the Description of their *Villas*, that the Architects, in the disposing of the several Members of them, had an Eye not only to the extraordinary Regularity observed by the *Romans* in forming their Camps, which *Polybius* so exactly describes, but even in some Measure to the very Manner of placing the several Officers and Servants belonging to Agriculture, the Master being lodged in that Part which bore the Name of the General's Pavilion, and the principal Servants in the Stations adjoining to their respective Charges.

Tho' the forementiond Authors on Agriculture agree, that almost all the same Members were necessary in all *Villas*, yet they differ in the Manner of disposing them. *Vitruvius* and *Palladius*, as has been before observed, mention but one Court, in the Middle of which the *Villa* was placed, but *Varro*, with whom *Columella* seems to agree, places the several Members of the *Villa* round an inner Court, and at the same Time had an outer Court surrounding the same *Villa*. The former Manner seems most proper for the small Farm, but the other where there was a larger Family with many Cattle and much Stores. Tho they differ in the Manner of disposing the *Villa*, yet they still agree in one Thing, that for the most Part the Men, Cattle, and Fruits were under one common Roof, and that the *Villa Rustica* and *Fructuaria* were join'd to the *Prætorium* by one common Wall. Tho' *Varro* gives us to understand that even in his Time it was sometimes otherwise, and indeed the Master's Part may be said to be more pleasant, when remov'd at a convenient Distance from the Stench of Cattle and other Nusances.

The Different Manners of disposing their *Villas* may be better understood by the following Draughts, the first of which, shews that of *Vitruvius* and *Palladius*, and the other, that of *Varro* and *Columella*

Thus

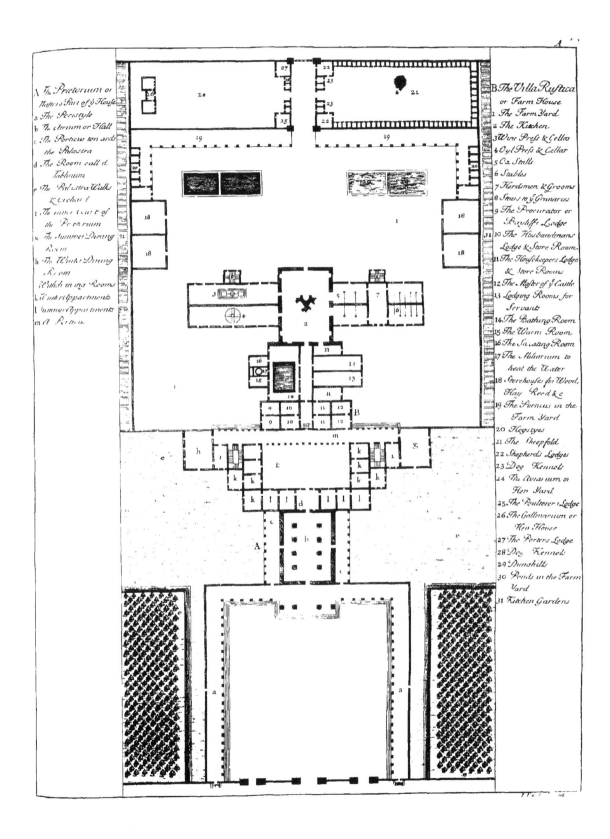

A

A *The Prætorium or Masters Part of y House*
a *The Peristyle*
b *The Atrium or Hall*
c *The Porticus toward the Palæstra*
d *The Room call'd Tablinum*
e *The Palæstra Walks & Orchard*
f *The inner court of the Prætorium*
g *The Summer Dining Room*
h *The Winter Dining Room*
i *Withdrawing Rooms*
k *Winter Appartments*
l *Summer Appartments*
m *A Portico*

B *The Villa Ruftica or Farm House*
1 *The Farm Yard*
2 *The Kitchen*
3 *Wine Preß & Cellar*
4 *Oyl Preß & Cellar*
5 *Ox Stalls*
6 *Stables*
7 *Herdsmen & Grooms*
8 *Stews to y Granaries*
9 *The Procurator or Bayliffs Lodge*
10 *The Husbandmans Lodge & Store Room*
11 *The Housekeepers Lodge & Store Rooms*
12 *The Master of y Cattle*
13 *Lodging Rooms for Servants*
14 *The Bathing Room*
15 *The Warm Room*
16 *The Sweating Room*
17 *The Miliarium to heat the Water*
18 *Storehouses for Wood, Hay Reed &c*
19 *The Porticus in the Farm Yard*
20 *Hogstyes*
21 *The Sheepfold*
22 *Shepherd's Lodges*
23 *Dog Kennels*
24 *The Aviarium or Hen Yard*
25 *The Poulterer's Lodge*
26 *The Gallinarium or Hen House*
27 *The Porters Lodge*
28 *Dog Kennels*
29 *Dunghills*
30 *Ponds in the Farm Yard*
31 *Kitchen Gardens*

Had not *Varro in lib. 4 de Lingua Latina*, inform'd us, that the military Word *Cohors* was originally a Word belonging to a *Villa*, I might have Reason to think, by the frequent Use made of that and *Prætorium* in the Description of their *Villas*, that the Architects, in the disposing of the several Members of them, had an Eye not only to the extraordinary Regularity observed by the *Romans* in forming their Camps, which *Polybius* so exactly describes, but even in some Measure to the very Manner of placing the several Officers and Servants belonging to Agriculture, the Master being lodged in that Part which bore the Name of the General's Pavilion, and the principal Servants in the Stations adjoining to their respective Charges.

Tho' the forementioned Authors on Agriculture agree, that almost all the same Members were necessary in all *Villas*, yet they differ in the Manner of disposing them. *Vitruvius* and *Palladius*, as has been before observed, mention but one Court, in the Middle of which the *Villa* was placed, but *Varro*, with whom *Columella* seems to agree, places the several Members of the *Villa* round an inner Court, and at the same Time had an outer Court surrounding the same *Villa*. The former Manner seems most proper for the small Farm, but the other where there was a larger Family with many Cattle and much Stores. Tho' they differ in the Manner of disposing the *Villa*, yet they still agree in one Thing, that for the most Part the Men, Cattle, and Fruits were under one common Roof, and that the *Villa Rustica* and *Fructuaria* were join'd to the *Prætorium* by one common Wall. Tho' *Varro* gives us to understand that even in his Time it was sometimes otherwise, and indeed the Master's Part may be said to be more pleasant, when remov'd at a convenient Distance from the Stench of Cattle and other Nusances.

The Different Manners of disposing their *Villas* may be better understood by the following Draughts, the first of which, shews that of *Vitruvius* and *Palladius*, and the other, that of *Varro* and *Columella*.

Thus

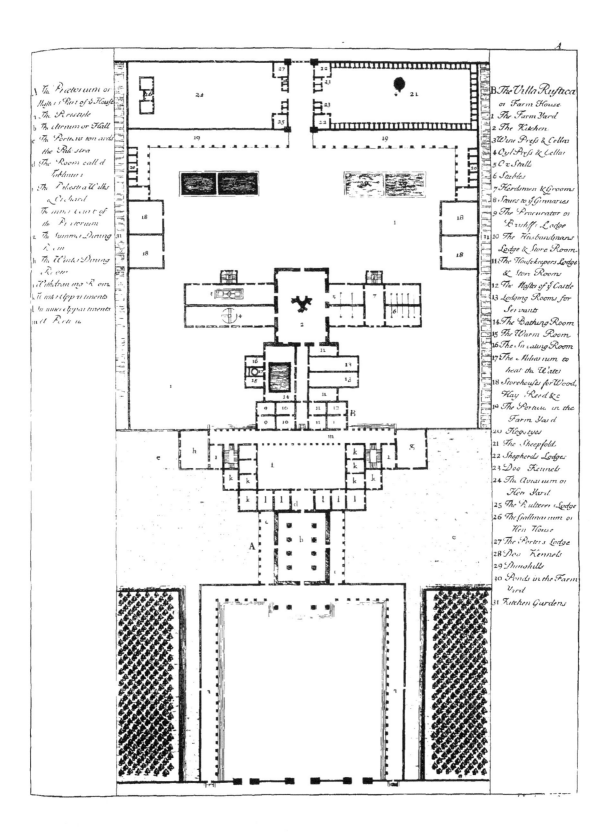

A The Pretorium or Master's Part of ye House
a The Peristyle
b The Atrium or Hall
c The Porticus toward the Palaestra
d The Room call'd Tablinum
e The Palaestra Walks & Orchard
f The inner court of the Pretorium
g The Summer Dining Room
h The Winter Dining Room
i With drawing Room
k Winter Apartments
l Summer Apartments
m The Portico

B The Villa Rustica or Farm House.
1 The Farm Yard
2 The Kitchen
3 Wine Press & Cellar
4 Oyl Press & Cellar
5 Ox Stalls
6 Stables
7 Herdsmen & Grooms
8 Stairs to ye Granaries
9 The Procurator or Bailiffs Lodge
10 The Husbandmans Lodge & Store Room
11 The Housekeepers Lodge & Store Rooms
12 The Master of ye Castle
13 Lodging Rooms for Servants
14 The Bathing Room
15 The Warm Room
16 The Sweating Room
17 The Milliarum to heat the Water
18 Storehouses for Wood, Hay, Reed &c
19 The Porticus in the Farm Yard
20 Hogsties
21 The Sheepfold
22 Shepherds Lodges
23 Dog Kennels
24 The Aviarium or Hen Yard
25 The Pulterer's Lodge
26 The Gallinarium or Hen House
27 The Porters Lodge
28 Dog Kennels
29 Dunghills
30 Ponds in the Farm Yard
31 Kitchen Gardens

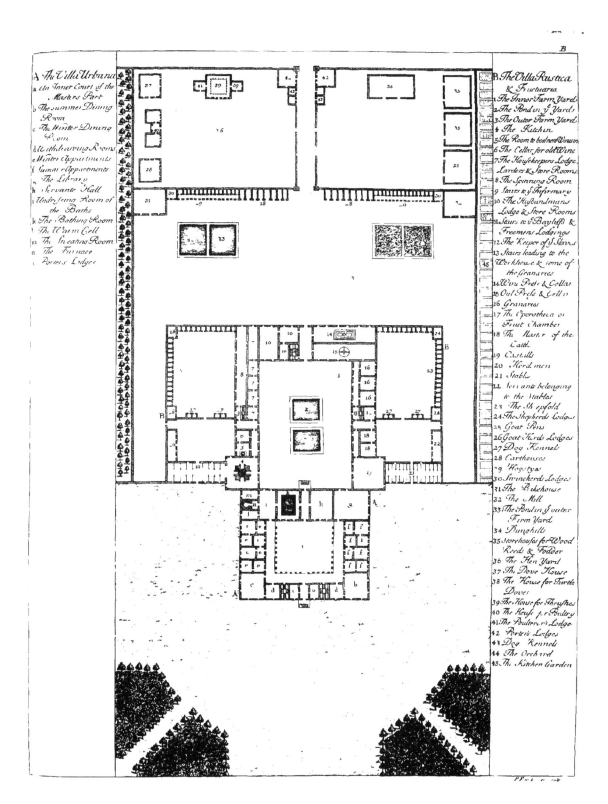

B

A The Villa Urbana
a An Inner Court of the Masters Part
b The summer Dining Room
c The Winter Dining Room
d Withdrawing Rooms
e Winter Appartments
f Summer Appartments
g The Library
h Servants Hall
i Undressing Room of the Baths
k The Bathing Room
l The Warm Cell
m The Sweating Room
n The Furnace
o Porters Lodge

B The Villa Rustica & Fructuaria
1 The Inner Farm Yard
2 The Pond in ye Yard
3 The Outer Farm Yard
4 The Kitchen
5 The Room to boil new Wines in
6 The Cellar for old Wine
7 The Housekeepers Lodge, Larders & Store Rooms
8 The Spinning Room
9 Stairs to ye Infirmary
10 The Husbandmans Lodge & Store Rooms
11 Stairs to ye Bayliffs & Freemens Lodgings
12 The Keeper of ye Stairs
13 Stairs leading to the Workhouse & some of the Granaries
14 Wine Prels & Cellar
15 Oyl Prels & Cellar
16 Granaries
17 The Operotheca or Fruit Chamber
18 The Master of the Cattle
19 Ostlers
20 Herdsmen
21 Stables
22 Servants belonging to the Stables
23 The Sheepfold
24 The Shepherds Lodges
25 Goat Pens
26 Goat Herds Lodges
27 Dog Kennels
28 Carthouses
29 Hogstyes
30 Swineherds Lodges
31 The Bakehouse
32 The Mill
33 The Pond in ye outer Farm Yard
34 Dunghills
35 Storehouses for Wood Reeds & Fodder
36 The Hen Yard
37 The Dove House
38 The House for Turtle Doves
39 The House for Thrushes
40 The House for Poultry
41 The Poulterers Lodge
42 Porters Lodges
43 Dog Kennels
44 The Orchard
45 The Kitchen Garden

P Fourdrinier sc.

Thus far have I endeavour'd to set forth the Rules that govern'd the Ancients in the Choice of Situations, and in placing the *Villa* properly, as also the Method obferved by their Architects in the Difpofition of every Member within the Circuit of the Farm-yard   There now remain only thofe Parts to be treated of, that were indeed dependent on the *Villa*, but for proper Reafons removed at a Diftance from it, as particularly thofe Places where the Beafts and Fowls were kept that are wild by Nature, or thrive not fo well when they have not Woods and Grafs Fields to range and feed in   The Cuftom of enclofing a Field for the Ufe of a Warren, was, as *Varro* intimates, *lib* 3 *cap* 4 in his Time of a very old ftanding among the *Romans*, but then as he alfo informs us *cap* 11 this *Leporarium* confifted but of one Acre of Ground, or two at moft, and contain'd in it nothing more than Hares and Rabbits But when this Author wrote, it appears that fome of them ufed to enclofe a great Number of Acres near their *Villas* for that Purpofe, in which fometimes other Sorts of Beafts were confin'd   The fame Author, in the Chapter immediately following, mentions a Piece of Ground of fifty Acres belonging to ℺ *Hortenfius*, call'd a *Therotrophium*, from being wholly appropriated to the Prefervation or Nourifhment of the larger Sort of wild Beafts, as Deer, Boars, wild Goats, &c It appears by *Columella*, who wrote not many Years after *Varro*, that tho the *Romans* in his Time had not alter'd their Cuftom of preferving feveral Sorts of Animals in Enclofures near their *Villas*, yet thus far they had alter'd it, that inftead of making two different Ones, *viz* one for Hares, and the other for other Sorts of Wild Beafts, they then confin'd them all in one Place, which they call'd the *Vivarium*, from the Number of living Creatures contain'd in it, and was the fame that we at prefent call a Park, in which were not only thofe feveral Sorts of Beafts before-mention'd, but alfo the Fowls that were kept without the Walls of the *Villa*, as well as Fifh Ponds   The Ground chofen for this Ufe, if the natural Situation of the Place allow'd of it, was productive of Grafs and thofe Trees that bore Acorns, Chefnuts or Maft, was well water'd by a Stream that ran through, and enclos'd either with Pales or a Wall, according to the Conveniency of the Country.

S

This

This was all the Care thought necessary concerning the Beasts there confin'd, but the Fowls requir'd further Care, and each Sort had Provision made for them suitable to their Natures. Of all which I shall give some Account from the Authority of the fore quoted Authors, beginning with the Peacocks, which *Columella, lib* 8 *cap* 11 says, *are best kept in small Islands, where they may wander at large free from the Danger of Robbers or Vermin. But such a Possession being very rare in inland Countries where they cannot be thus preserved, a grassy woody Field must be enclos'd by an high Wall, on three Sides whereof must be a* Porticus, *and on the fourth two Cells, one for the Keepers, and the other the Pens for the Peacocks. Then under the* Porticus *must be ranged in order Fences of Reeds, like those on the Tops of Pidgeon-Houses, these Fences must be divided by Reeds intermix'd like Bars, so that they may have different Passages from each Side.* In the subsequent Chapter the same Author tells us, that the same Means that were observed in bringing up Peacocks were also observed with Turkeys. The Disposition of the Place which was made for Geese to breed in, and call'd *Chenoboscion* by *Columella,* is by him *lib* 8. *cap* 14 describ'd in the following Manner. *The Yard must be kept shut close from any other Sort of Fowl, surrounded with a Wall nine Feet high, and a Porticus, so that the Keepers Lodge may be in some Part of it. Under the Porticus are to be square Pens built with Mortar or Bricks large enough for each to have three Feet every Way, and each Passage secur'd with little Doors, because upon Account of their breeding they ought to be carefully penn'd up, and that without the Villa. If there is a Pond or River not far from the House, no other Water is requir'd, but if not, a Pond must be dug for the Fowls to wash themselves in, for they can no more live without Water than without Land. A marshy and grassy Ground must be allotted them, and other Sorts of Food sown, such as Vetches, three leaved Grass and Fænugreek, but especially that kind of Succory which the* Greeks *call* Seris By the Description that both *Varro* and *Columella* give of the *Neossotrophion,* it appears to have been well guarded to hinder the Flight of those several Species of wild web footed Fowl that were confin'd within it, and is in none of the Authors on Country Affairs is to be found any Provision for the breeding of tame Ducks, we must be content

tent with the Directions which are deliver'd most largely to us by *Columella, lib 8 cap 15* about the *Neossotrophion* in these Words *A plain Place is to be chosen and fenced with a Wall fifteen Feet high, then Lattices are placed on it, or else it is cover'd with Nets that have strong Meshes, that the Fowls within may not flye out, nor the Haukes or Eagles fly in* But the whole *Wall is to be plaster'd without and within, that Cats or Serpents may not enter* In the Middle of the Neossotrophion, *a Pond is to be dug two Feet deep, and as long and broad as the Place will allow* The Mouth of the Pond, *that it may not be broken down by the Violence of the Water, which ought always to flow within it, must be plaster'd, and not rais'd by Steps, but decline a little, that the Fowl may descend as it were from a shelving Shore into the Water* The Ground round the Pond *must be paved with Stone near two thirds of the Bounds, and cover'd with Plaister, that the Grass may not sprout out, and the Surface of the Water be clear for them to swim in* Again, the Middle Part *must be Land, that it may be planted with Egyptian Beans and other Greens that usually grow in Water, which may shade the Fowls Haunts* For *some delight to lodge in Thickets of Tamarisk or Stalks of Flags, yet the whole Place is not for that Reason to be taken up with Thickets, but, as I said before, there must be none round the Banks, that the Fowls, when sporting in the Heat of the Day, may without any Hindrance strive which swims fastest, for as they are glad to have Holes to creep into, and where they may catch the Insects that lurk upon the Water, so they are offended if there is not a free Passage out of the Pond, wherefore the Bank should be cover'd all round with Grass for twenty Feet, and behind the Bounds of this Ground round a Wall must be Holes, where the Fowls are to build their Nests, a Foot square made of Stone and Plaister, and cover'd with Shrubs of Box or Myrtle intermix'd, not exceeding the height of the Wall* Next there *must be a Channel of running Water sunk in the Ground, through which the Meat mix'd with the Water, may constantly run, for thus does that kind of Fowls feed*

That the *Romans* took Care also to breed Pheasants, Partridge and other Birds, may be collected from several of their Authors, but as we have no particular Account of the Manner observed, I shall omit to speak of them, and only take Notice of what other Buildings they commonly had within their larger Parks, which were of two

Sorts the first for the Conveniences and Lodgings of the Hunters, Fowlers, Fishermen, and Keepers, and the other for the Retirement and Pleasure of the Master of the *Villa*, such as the *Triclinium, Museum*, and *Ornithon*, all which are mention'd by *Varro* in his third Book, in the 12 Chapter of which he speaks of the *Triclinium*, that was in the Middle of the Park, already mention'd, that *Hortensius* had near *Laurentia*, where *Pliny's Villa* was afterwards built. And in the 4ᵗʰ Chapter of the same Book, after giving an Account of the *Ornithon* of *Strabo* near *Brundusium*, and that of *Lucullus* at *Tusculum*, he proceeds to mention the *Museum* and *Ornithon* he had himself near his *Villa* by *Cassinum*, and as he has been very ample in the Description of the latter, which in his Time was reckon'd a Master piece of its kind, I shall give the Translation of his own Words at large, and endeavour the Explanation of them before I proceed to speak of the other Things that were near their *Villas*.

There a Canal under the Town Cassinum, *which runs clear and deep by my Villa, fifty seven Feet broad, with Stone Banks, and there is a Passage by Bridges from one Villa to the other, the length is nine hundred and fifty Feet from an Island made by the River* Vinius *to the* Museum, *where flows another River to the upper Part of the Canal where the* Museum *stands. About the Banks of which is an open Walk ten Feet broad, from this Walk towards the Fields, the Place of the* Ornithon *is enclos'd on each Side on the Right and Left with high Walls, betwixt which the* Ornithon *extends its Breadth forty eight Feet in the Shape of a Writing Table with a Head, the square Part is in Length seventy two Feet, the round Part which is the Capital is twenty seven Feet. Moreover, as a Walk is describ'd at the Bottom*

---

¹ *Flua.*] The different Names that *Varro* gives to the several Bodies of Water about his *Villa*, require that we take Notice of his Explanation of them, lib 4 *de Lingua Latina*, where he says, that *Lacus* signifies a large Trench where Water may be contain'd, *Palus* a shallow Water usually intituled *Stagnum*, call'd by the Greeks *Stagnon*, was a round Bason of Water, *Fluvius* and *Flumen* that which constantly flows, *Amnis* is that running Water that surrounds any Thing, *Amnis* being deriv'd from *Ambitus*.

² *Museum*] The Name of any Place sacred to the Muses, and seems to have meant a Place proper for Retirement and Study, rather than only a Repository for Books, which *Bibliotheca* literally means.

³ *Ornithon*] Is generally us'd by *Varro* to signify a Place where Birds of several kinds are kept, for tho' that were kept separate had Buildings call'd after the Names of the Fowls there confin'd.

of

a	Two high Walls	e	Alcoves in ỹ Parterre	i	The Porticus	n	a Small Field Table
b	Walks about ỹ Omathon	f	a Walk from ỹ Alcove to ỹ Area	k	The Plan of ỹ Tholus	o	The Bed for ỹ Guest
c	The Area	g	Two Ponds	l	Water within ỹ Pillars	p	The place for ỹ Birds
d	ê l Parterre	h	The Path betwixt ỹ Ponds	m	The Margin to ỹ same	q	a Regular plant ô Wood

P I out de mier sculp

a	The outer Pillars of Stone	l	A small Island
b	Small Pillars of Tin	m	The Pillar supporting the Table
c	Nets between the outer Pillars	n	The indicated Wheel or Table
d	Bird Net over the small Pillars	o	The Tholus or Cupola
e	Perche between the Nets	p	The Horologe within ye Hemisphere
f	Stone work at the Back of the Falere	q	The Star Lucifer
g	The Falere or Bed of Stone	r	The Circle of ye Winds & its Index
h	The Cubature Place to walk on	s	The Wind Fane
i	Ducks Nests in ye under part of ye Falere	t	The Stylobata of the Pillars
k	The Pond within the Falere	u	The foot Margin of the Pond

P. Fourdrinier sculp.

of the Table, as a Margin, *without the* Ornithon *is a* [4] Parterre, *in the Middle whereof are Alcoves, by which is a Way to the* Area. *In the Entrance is a* Porticus *on the Right and Left, with Dwarf Trees placed betwixt the Stone Pillars of the first Row from the Top of the Wall to the Architrave, an hempen Net serves for a Covering to the* Porticus, *and from the Architrave to the Pedestal it is fill'd with all Sorts of Birds, which are fed through the Net, and the Water flows through in a small Stream. Adjoining to the inner Part of the Pedestal, on each Side the upper Part of the square* Area, *are two oblong Fish Ponds opposite to the* Porticus, *between the two Ponds is the only Path leading to the* [5] Tholus, *which is a round Colonade as in the Temple of* Catullus, *provided you make Pillars instead of Walls. On the outside of the Pillars is a Wood regularly planted, cover'd with great Trees, that the lower Parts may be seen through, the whole is surrounded with high Walls. Within the outer Pillars of the* Tholus, *and the like Number of small inner Pillars of Fir there is a place five Feet broad; between the outer Pillars are Nets instead of a Wall, that the Grove may be seen, and to hinder the Birds that are there from flying out. Within the inner Pillars there is a Bird's Net instead of a Wall, between these and the outer Pillars are Benches like a small Theatre, with many Pearches for Birds upon every Pillar. Within the Nets are all Sorts of Birds, especially singing Birds, as the Nightingal and Black-Bird, which receive their Water by a small Trough, and their Meat is thrown under the Net. Below the Pedestal of the Pillars, is a Stone a Foot and half high from the* [6] Falere. *The* Falere *it self is two Feet high from the Pond and five Feet broad, that the*

---

[4] *Plumula*] Cl *Salmasius* in his Notes on *Vopiscus* says, that the Ancients gave that Name to those round Marks of Gold and Purple made in the Shape of Feathers, with which their Garments were mark'd and diversify'd. They also gave the Name of *Plumæ* to those round Plates and circular Irons out of which their *Briganines* were hammer'd, because they bore the Likeness of Feathers; as also some were call'd *Squamæ*, because like the Scales of Fishes. *Vitruvius, lib* 6 *cap* 7 calls Embroidery or Needle-work *Plumariorum textura*, which being imitated by the Gardiners of that Time, and they wanting a Name for the Curlings they made of Box-Hedges or the like on the Ground, from their Imitation it is not unlikely they gave them the Name of *Plumæ* or *Plumulæ*, which we from the *French* call *Parterres*.

[5] *Tholus* appears by *Vitruvius* to mean the hemispherical Covering of a Building, tho' sometimes, as in this Place, it was used to signify the whole Building so cover'd.

[6] *Falere*] By *Varro*'s Account *Falere* signify'd the same which afterwards in *Pliny*'s Time was call'd *Stibadium*, and was a fix'd Bed of Stone for dining on in some Building distant from the *Villa*.

Guests may walk upon the Culcita *round by the small Pillars, and the Bottom within the* Falere *is a Pond with a Margin to walk upon, and a small Island in the Middle, round the* Falere *and the Pond are hollow'd Pens for Ducks   In the Island is a small Pillar, in the Inside of which is an* AXIS *supporting a radiated Wheel instead of a Table, so that at the End, where the Circle of the Wheel is generally sharp, the Table is made hollow like a Drum, two Feet and an half broad, and nine Inches deep, this is so turned by a By-stander, that all the Provision of Meat and Drink may be served up at once to the Guests   From the* Suggestum *of the* Falere, *where the Hangings usually are, the Ducks come forth into the Pond and swim, whence a little Stream runs into the two Fish Ponds abovemention'd, and the Fishes swim to and fro   Likewise by the turning of certain Cocks, both hot Water and cold is convey'd to each of the Guests, from the wooden Orb and Table abovemention'd   Within, under the* Tholus *the Star* Lucifer *by Day,* Hesperus *in the Night, make their Revolutions to the lower Part of the Hemisphere, so as to set with them   In the Middle of the same Hemisphere, round a Point is the Circle of the eight Winds, as at* Athens *on the Dial made by* Cyrrestes, *and a little Hand reaching from the Point to the Orb, is so moved as to touch the Wind which blows, and notify the same to those that are within*

In the Description of all the other Places for Fowls, both in *Varro* and *Columella* it may be observed, that their whole Care has been how to dispose Things properly for the breeding young ones, or fattening those contain'd in them   But in this, as it was chiefly fill'd with singing Birds, regard was had to Pleasure, not forgetting at the same Time to make the Restraint of the Birds as little irksome as possible, but it may be still observed, that even here some Regard was had to

Culcita] As *Lectus* signify'd the Bed which the Guests rock up with the breadth of their Backs, so *Culcita* was that Part below on which the Waters stood, or the Guests walk'd on to their respective Places, and was nothing, as here, upon a Level with the Bed itself *Varro, speaking of an eating Place, calls this Place Culcina, and says it was so call'd, because on that Part was laid the Mat or Carpet, or any thing that was trodden on, Culcita being so call'd also*

Suggestum is most commonly used to signify the solid Bank of Earth, or Bed of Stones, on which the General stood when he made an Oration to his Soldiers in the Camp, and as this was the solid Part of the *Falere*, it was call'd by the same Name, since it could not be properly call'd the *Podium* or *Stylobata*, which always had Pillars or something else fix'd on them

Profit

Profit, for we find Care taken for the bringing up Ducks: And tho'
the Description does not in many Respects answer that of the *Neossotrophion* beforemention'd, yet there are some Parts of it that do, as the
Ponds, the Nests under the *Tholus*, and the Covering of Nets to prevent their Flight But there are two Things still more particular to be
observed in this Passage of *Varro*, viz the first mention of a *Parterre* by
any *Roman* Author, and what is more worthy our Notice, an elegant
Description of, perhaps, the first Clock that was ever made in *Italy*,
that measur'd the Hours of the Day and Night by an Hand, which was
wholly mov'd by Clock work, as this appears to have been And 'tis
not impossible but *Varro* might have been the Inventor of it, he living
not long after *Scipio Nasica*, who *Pliny* the Naturalist, *lib* 7 *cap* 60.
says, was the first Inventor of Clocks that measur'd the Time by Water, and we find that he kill'd *Caius Gracchus* in the Year 621 of the
City, and our Author wrote about the Time of the first *Triumvirate*.
The Circle of the eight Winds, and Index that was on the Top of the
Hemisphere, was by his Account founded on an *Athenian* Invention,
and seems to have been much admir'd by the Artists of his Time.
For tho' his Cotemporary *Vitruvius* calls the Author of it *Cyrrhestes*,
it is plain he speaks of the same Invention, *lib* 1 *cap* 6 which he thus
describes Andronicus Cyrrhestes *built a Marble* Octogon *Tower at*
Athens, *and in every Side of the* Octogon *appointed the Image of a Wind
to be carved against the Points from whence it blew, and upon that Tower
made a Marble Cone, whereon he put a brazen* Triton, *holding a Wand in
his Right hand And it was so contrived as to turn with the Wind, and always stand opposite to the Wind that blew, and hold the pointing Wand
over the Image of that Wind* The seeming Difference that appears
in the Account of these two Authors in speaking of this Invention, (viz that one calls it *Horologium* and the other *Turris)* may be
thus reconcil'd, if we may be allow'd to suppose that this *Turris* was
made a *Gnomon* to one of those *Sun Dials* that, as appears by *Vitruvius*
and *Pliny* the Naturalist, were placed on the Ground in some publick
Place of all the Cities of the Ancients, as that in *Rome* was in the
Campus Martius, whose *Gnomon*, which was an *Obelisk*, I think was not
more proper than this, which at the same Time serv'd for the Uses
before-

beforemention'd The Cone that was on the Top being that Part of the *Gnomon,* that ſerved to point out the Hour The Body of this Building remaining at preſent entire, may be ſeen in Sir G *Wheeler's* Travels. *Varro* indeed differs very materially from this Invention of *Cyrrheſtes,* in that of his Wind-Fane, making his Index move within the Hemiſphere But he pretends to no more than that he took from this *Grecian* the Method of dividing the Quarters of the Heavens into eight Winds, which appears by the foremention'd Chapter of *Vitruvius* to have been at that Time newly invented

To proceed to the *Villa* It is neceſſary here to take Notice, that beſides the Proviſion for Fowls and Beaſts, the *Romans* were not leſs mindful to have near their *Villas,* where the Situation would allow, Ponds both of freſh and ſalt Water, preferring ſtill the latter, on which they beſtowed no ſmall Coſt, as may be ſeen by *Plutarch's* Deſcription of thoſe of *Lucullus* near *Miſenum,* and may be alſo collected from the Rules given by *Varro* and *Columella* for making them, with proper Retirements for the Fiſh during extream hot or cold Weather

Nearer the *Villa* than the *Vivarium,* and adjoining to the Walls of the Farm-yard, were the Orchard and Kitchen Garden, in or near which it appears by *Varro,* that it was cuſtomary in his Time to have Places allotted for the Preſervation of Snails and Dormice, both of which are often mention'd by *Apicius* in his Account of the *Roman* Cookery And the Places in which they were kept, call'd *Cochleare* and *Gliarium* by *Varro,* are thus deſcrib'd by him *lib* 3 *cap* 14 *A proper Place in the open Air is to be provided to preſerve Snails in, which you muſt encompaſs all round with Water, that you may find thoſe you put there to breed, as well as their young ones, I ſay they are to be encompaſs'd with Water, that they may have no Opportunity of eſcaping That is the moſt convenient Place which is not ſcorched by the Sun, and yet refreſh'd by the Dew, as it ſeldom is in a ſunny Place However, don't put them too much in the Shade, as under Rocks and Mountains whoſe Feet are waſh'd by Lakes and Rivers, the Place may be made dewy by bringing in a Pipe and putting ſmall Cocks into it, which ſhall eject the Water ſo as to make it fall upon ſome Stone and diffuſe itſelf widely The*

The Glirarium *is managed in a different Manner, because the Place is not surrounded with Water, but Walls The whole is cover'd with Stone or Plaister within to hinder the Dormice from creeping out There ought to be little Trees in it that may bear Acorns, but when they don't bear Fruit, you must throw within the Walls Acorns and Chesnuts for them to feed upon You must make large Holes for them to breed in, there ought to be but a small Quantity of Water, because they don't use much and require a dry Place*

The extraordinary Service that Bees were to Mankind, was the Cause that an Apiary was thought absolutely necessary to be near most of the Ancient *Villas,* and the wonderful Care they took in breeding them may be seen in the several Authors *de Rebus Rusticis,* who have all spoken very largely on this Head, but particularly *Columella* and *Virgil,* the first having thought it worthy of being the Subject of almost his whole 9 Book, and the latter has employ'd the greatest Part of his 4th *Georgic* in describing the several wonderful Qualities of that industrious Insect, whose Description of the *Apiary,* as it contains every Thing that other Authors have wrote on that Head, on Account of its Elegancy I shall prefer before them, and insert it here as it is translated by the Earl of *Lauderdale*

First, for your Bees a quiet Station find,
Debar'd Access of th'all infulting Wind,
Winds hinder them then liquid Sweets to bear,
Through stormy Tracts of violated Air
Their Haunts secure from sporting Kids and
    Sheep,
Who Morning Dew from Flowers and Blossoms
    sweep,
As wanton Heifers, feeding through the Fields,
Tread down the Blooms the springing Pasture yields
Muskets and other Birds infest the Hive
In from your Bees enamell'd Lizards drive
The Swallows catch them flying, then convey
To their expecting Young the luscious Prey
    Let crystal Fountains all your Hives surround,
And living Springs glide thro' the flowry Ground,
Or purling Rills creep thro' the Grass unseen,
With mossy Pools all matted o'er with Green.

Before the Entry let wild Olives spread,
Or Palms diffuse around a grateful Shade,
That, when the Kings their new form'd Squa-
    drons bring,
To take the Pleasures of the friendly Spring,
They on the Banks may find a cool Retreat,
Shelter'd by Leaves from scorching Phœbus'
    Heat
Whither your Waters stand in Pools or flow,
Across them Stones or willow Branches throw
When Rain or takes them lingering in the Woods,
Or Wind hath cast them headlong in the Floods,
The Bees will on these frequent Bridges stand,
And to the Sun their glittering Wings expand
The verdant Lavender must there abound,
That Savory shed its pleasant sweets around,
There Beds of purple Violets should bloom,
And fragrant Thyme the ambient Air perfume

U

Varro,

Varro, to whom we are chiefly indebted for the many Lights we have receiv'd for the Disposition of several principal Parts in and about the ancient *Villas*, has also in the beginning of his Work acquainted us with the Mythology of the *Roman* Husbandmen, where, without mentioning the famous scare-crow God of the Gardens, he reckons up no less than twelve that were properly on several Occasions worship'd by the Countryman. The two first were *Jupiter* and *Tellus*, that were esteem'd the two great Parents of all Things. The next were *Sol* and *Luna*, the Governours of Times and Seasons. *Bacchus* and *Ceres* were worship'd, because they furnish'd those Fruits that were most necessary for the Support of Life. To *Robigus* they addrels'd their Prayers to guard their Fruits from Blasts, and to *Flora* that they may flourish in Season. *Minerva* was look'd upon as the Guardian of the Olive Grounds, and *Venus* of the Gardens. The Goddess of Waters requir'd to be particularly address'd to, that their Tillage might not suffer through Droughts, and the God called *Bonus Eventus*, that their Labours might meet with Success. Of these twelve Deities, she that was principally worship'd was *Ceres*, whose Temple and Statue were immediately under the Care of the principal Man in each Province, as we may conjecture from the 29th Epistle of *Pliny* in the 9th Book, in which he gives Directions to his Architect to repair the Temple of that Goddess, which as it may serve something to illustrate some Passages of their Country Religion, I shall give it entire. *By the Advice of the South-sayers, I must rebuild the Temple of* Ceres *on my Estate in a better Manner, being old and very close when throng'd on any set Day. For many People meet there on the Ides of* September *from all Parts of the Country. Many Affairs are transacted, many Vows are made, and others paid, but there is no place near for Shelter from the Rain or Sun, it will therefore appear both munificent and religious, if to the Temple which I shall build very handsomely I add a* Porticus, *that for the Use of the Goddess, this for the Service of Man. I would have you therefore buy some Marble Pillars of what Sort you shall think best, and also Marble to encrust the Throne and Walls. I will also have an Image of the Goddess either made or bought, because the old one of Wood is in some Parts decay'd through Age. As to the* Porticus *there is Occasion to say nothing more of it but that you draw out*

the

the Form of it according as the Place allows, only it cannot be Bounds for the Temple, for the Ground on which that stands is encompass'd on one side with the River and broken Banks, and on the other by a Road. There is beyond the Road a large Meadow, in which the Porticus will be sufficiently manifest against the Temple, unless you, who are wont by Art to overcome the Difficulties of Places, can find out a better expedient.

If the *Romans* (which with Justice cannot be believ'd) ever divided Architecture into two Branches, and had separate Professors for City and Country Buildings, I believe, by what has been already said, it does not appear that the Studies of those who profess'd the latter, requir'd less Care and Judgment than the former, for it may be observed, that in the Choice of a Situation for a *Villa* there was as much Knowledge of Nature requir'd, as in that for a City. And if those Buildings that were in Cities rais'd for publick Conveniences, Religion or Diversions, were necessarily more magnificent, and requir'd the Knowledge of some particular Things not necessary to the Country Architect, yet the latter, in the Care he was oblig'd to take in providing for all Things that were dependent on Agriculture, had certainly as many different Things to look to not needful to be known by the Architect that was wholly employ'd in the Buildings of the City.

In the former Part of this Work I have endeavour'd to set forth, by the Example of one of *Pliny*'s *Villas*, the Method observed by an ancient Architect in the Disposition of a *Villa Urbana*, situated in *Italy* on the *Mediterranean* Sea. In this second Part, from the Authority of several *Roman* Authors, I have shewn the Rules that were observed when the Farm House was contiguous to the Master's Part. There now remains the *Tuscan Villa* of *Pliny* to be spoken of, which shall be the Subject of the following Part of this Work. But that I may make every Thing I treat of appear as intelligible as possible, before I proceed any further, I think proper to shew by a Draught, the Disposition of the *Villa* treated on in this second Part with its *Limitations*. Which I have endeavour'd to do from the foregoing Rules, and by placing the *Villa* in the Manner *Varro* mentions, in the Beginning of the Description of his *Ornithon*.

A *The*

A *The* Prætorium

B *The* Farm House *and Buildings adjoining*

C *A Canal parting the Farm from the* Prætorium

D *Stone Banks to the Canal*

E *Bridges between the* Villas

F *The* Museum *at the Head of the Canal*

G *The River* Vinius

H *Part of the Island surrounded by that River*

I *The other River*

K *The* Walk *on the* Bank *of that* River.

L *The* Ornithon *of* Varro

M *The* Vivarium

N *Small woody Islands for Peacocks*

O *A Place for Turkeys and their Keeper*

P *For Geese and their Keeper*

Q *A Place to preserve Snails in*

R *For Dormice*

S *The Apiary*

T *The Threshing Floor and Barn*

U *The Mill*

W *The Temple of* Ceres

a *Cornfields*

b *Vineyards*

c *Olive-Grounds.*

d *Meadows*

e *Orchard*

f *Garden*

g *Osier Ground*

h 1 *Woods and Coppice*

THE

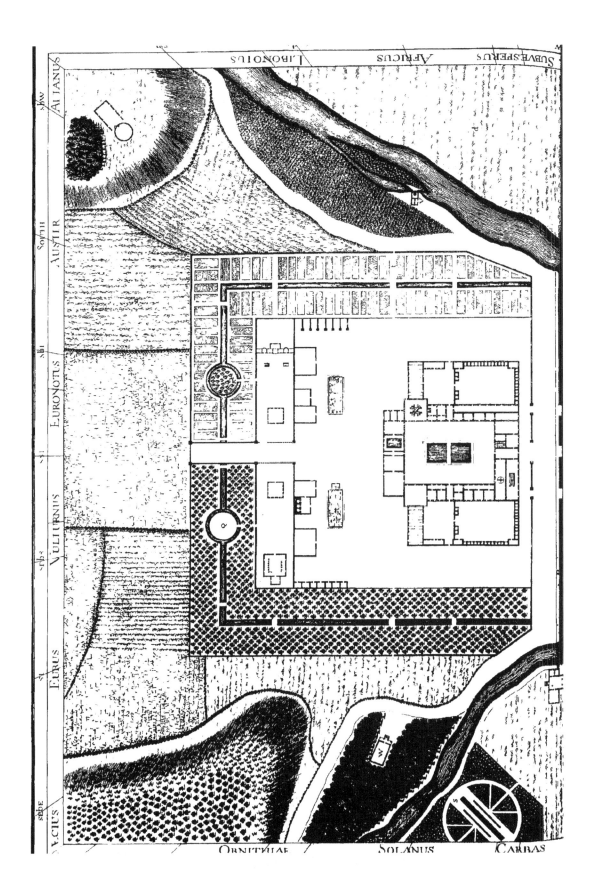

SUBVESPERUS AFRICUS LIBONOTUS

ALTANUS

AUSTER

EURONOTUS

VULTURNUS

EURUS

EACIUS

ORNITHIAE SOLANUS CARBAS

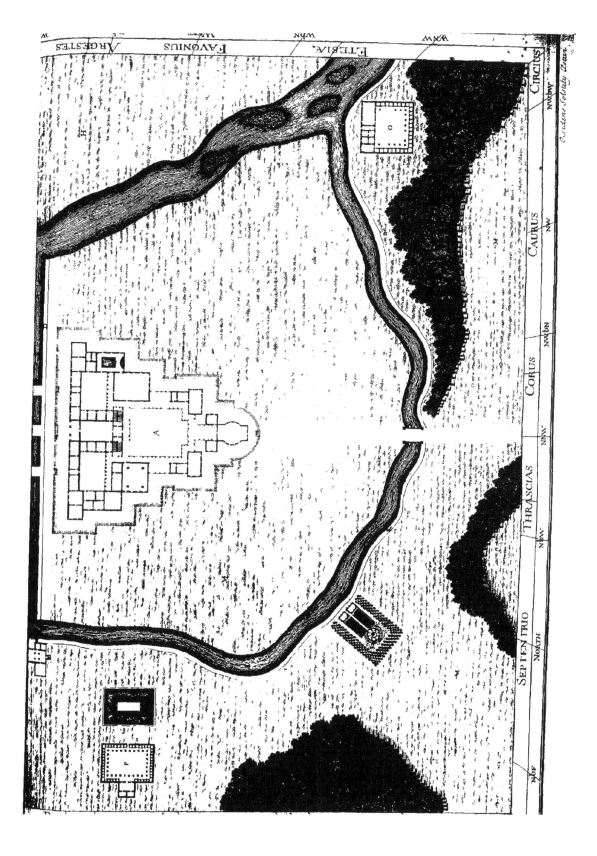

SEPTENTRIO   THRASCIAS   CORUS   CAURUS   CIRCIUS

ARGESTES   FAVONIUS   ETESIA.

THE
VILLAS of the ANCIENTS
ILLUSTRATED.

PART III.

The Description contain'd in the following Epistle, is of a Villa of Pliny's near a Town call'd Tifernum Tiberinum in Tuscany, as he informs us lib 4 epist 24 and if it was on the same I ana he mentions lib 10 epist 24 it lay near 150 Miles from Rome, or, to use his own Words, beyond the 150th Stone This Villa Pliny has taken frequent Occasion to mention in Letters to his Friends, and it may be observed, that he always writes of it as his principal Seat, and in lib 3 epist 19 takes Notice of a large Estate that lay round it, and doubtless had Provision for all the Conveniencies of Life near him, tho' he neglects to speak of them In the Account of this Villa there will be Occasion to observe, that Pliny considers it in a Manner very different from that of Laurentinum, not only with respect to the Situation, but to the House itself, it being, as he informs us lib 9 epist 36 his constant Residence in the Summer Season

### LIB. V. EP VI	### BOOK V EP. VI.
C. Plinius Apollinari suo, S.	Pliny *to* Apollinaris, *Health.*

AMAVI Curam & Sollicitudinem tuam, qui cum audisses me Æstate Thuscos meos petiturum, ne facerem suasisti, dum putas insalubres Est sane gravis & pestilens Ora Thusco-

Was pleas'd with the Regard and Uneasiness you express'd, when you heard I design'd to pass the Summer at my Seat in Tuscany, since you thought that Country unhealthy I acknowledge that the

X   Air

Thufcorum, quæ per Littus extenditur fed hi procul à Marte celebrant, quinetiam Apennino faluberrimo Montium frequent Atque adeo, ut omnem pro me Metum ponas, accipe Temperiem Cœli, Regionis Situm, Villæ Amœnitatem, quæ & tibi audita, & mihi relatu jucunda erunt Cœlum eft Hyeme frigidum & gelidum Myrtos, Oleas, quæque alia affiduo Tepore lætantur, afpernatur ac refpuit Laurum tamen patitur, atque etiam viridiffimam profert, interdum, fed non fæpius quam fub Urbe noftra, necat Æftatis mira Clementia, femper Aer Spiritu aliquo movetur, frequentius tamen Auras quam Ventos habet hinc Senes multos videas Avos, Proavofque jam Juvenum, audias Fabulas veteres, Sermonetque Majorum cumque veneris illo, putes alio te Sæculo natum Regionis forma pulcherrima Imaginare Amphitheatrum aliquod immenfum, & quale fola Rerum Natura poffit effingere Lata & diffufa Planities Montibus cingitur Montes fumma fui Parte procera Nemora & antiqua habent, fic

Air of the Sea Coaft of Tuscany is that and infectious But this Place is fo remov'd from the Sea, and lies even under the moft healthful of Mountains the Apennines But that you may lay afide all Fears for me, let me defcribe to you the Temperatenefs of the Climate, the Situation of the Country, and the Delightfulnefs of my Villa, which will be as agreeable to you to hear as to me to relate The Climate is cold and frofty in Winter fo that the Myrtles, Olives, and other Trees that require a continual Warmth, will not thrive here However it admits the Laurel, and produces the moft green and flourifhing, which yet fometimes, tho not oftner than about Rome, it deftroys. The Clemency of the Summer is wonderful, and the Air which is always in fome Motion, is more frequently ftirred by Breezes than by Winds hence you fee feveral old Men Grandfires, and great Grandfires to adult Perfons, and hear the old Stories, and Sentences of their Forefathers So that when you come there, you would think you had your felf been born in another Age The Face of the Country is very beautiful imagine to your felf a vaft Amphitheatre, which only the Hand of Nature herfelf could form, being a wide extended plain furrounded with Mountains whofe Tops are cover'd with lofty

frequens ibi & varia Venatio: inde cæduæ Sylvæ cum ipso Monte descendunt: has inter pingues, terrenique Colles, (neque enim facile usquam Saxum, etiam si quæratur, occurrit,) planissimis Campis Fertilitate non cedunt; opimamque Messem serius tantum, sed non minus percoquunt Sub his per latus omne Vineæ porriguntur, u-namque Faciem longè lateque contexunt· quarum à Fine, imoque quasi Margine, Arbusta nascuntur· Prata inde, Campique Campi, quos nonnisi ingentes Boves & fortissimi Aratri perfringunt tantis Glebis tenacissimum Solum, cum primum proscetur, assurgit, ut nono demum Sulco perdometur Prata florida & gemmea, Trifolium, aliasque Herbis, teneras semper & molles, & quasi novas alunt; cuncta enim perennibus Rivis nutriuntur Sed ubi Aquæ plurimum, Palus ruit, quia devexa Terra quicquid Liquoris accepit, nec absorbuit, effundit in Tiberim Medios ille Agros secat· Nivium patiens, omnesque Fruges devehit in Urbem;

lofty ancient *Woods*; *which give opportunity to frequent and various sorts of Hunting From thence the Under-woods descend with the Mountains intermixt with these are small Hills, of a strong fat Soil, (and where tho' sought, a Stone can scarcely be found) and which for Fruitfulness do not yield to the most level Fields; their Harvest is indeed somewhat later, but not less Under these Hills the Vineyards extend themselves on every side, and together form one long spacious View their Extremities and Bottoms, are bounded as it were by a Border of Shrubs below these are Meadows and Fields The Fields, such as require the largest Oxen and strongest Ploughs the stiff Soil, when first stirred, rising in such clods, that it is not sufficiently broken till it has been plow'd nine times The Meadows are flowery and budding, producing the Trefoil, and other Herbs, fresh and as it were always springing, as being nourished by ever-flowing Rivulets but tho there be much, there is no standing Water, because as the Ground lies shelving, whatever Water it receives, and does not imbibe, it throws into the Tiber This River divides the Land and in Winter and Spring is navigable, and*

Thuscorum, quæ per Littus extenditur sed hi procul ... cesserant, quinetiam Apennino ... saluberrimo Montium subjacent Atque ideo, ut omnem pro me Metum ponas, accipe Temperiem Cæli, Regionis Situm, Villæ Amoenitatem, quæ & tibi audita, & mihi relatu jucunda erunt Cœlum est Hyeme frigidum & gelidum Myrtos, Oleas, quæque alia assiduo Tepore lætantur, aspernatur ac respuit Laurum tamen patitur, atque etiam viridissimam profert, interdum, sed non sæpius quam sub Urbe nostra, necat Æstatis mira Clementia, semper Aer Spiritu aliquo movetur, frequentius tamen Auras quam Ventos habet hinc Senes multos videas Avos, Proavosque jam Juvenum, audias Fabulas veteres, Sermonesque Majorum cumque veneris illo, putes alio te Sæculo natum Regionis Forma pulcherrima Imaginare Amphitheatrum aliquod immensum, & quale sola Rerum Natura possit effingere Lata & diffusa Planities Montibus cingitur Montes summa sui Parte procera Nemora & antiqua habent, fre-

An of the Sea Coast of Tuscany is thick and infectious But this Place is far removed from the Sea, and lies even under the most healthful of Mountains the Apennines But that you may lay aside all Fears for me, let me describe to you the Temperateness of the Climate, the Situation of the Country, and the Delightfulness of my Villa, which will be as agreeable to you to hear as to me to relate The Climate is cold and frosty in Winter so that the Myrtles, Olives, and other Trees that require a continual Warmth, will not thrive here However it admits the Laurel, and produces the most green and flourishing, which yet sometimes, tho' not oftner than about Rome, it destroys. The Clemency of the Summer is wonderful, and the Air which is always in some Motion, is more frequently stirred by Breezes than by Winds hence you see several old Men Grandsires, and great Grandsires to adult Persons, and hear the old Stories, and Sentences of their Forefathers So that when you come there, you would think you had your self been born in another Age The Face of the Country is very beautiful imagine to your self a vast Amphitheatre, which only the Hand of Nature herself could form, being a wide extended plain surrounded with Mountains whose Tops are cover'd with lofty

frequens ibi & varia Venatio. inde
cæduæ Sylvæ cum ipso Monte descendunt · has inter pingues, terrenique Colles, (neque enim facile
usquam Saxum, etiam si quæratur,
occurrit,) planissimis Campis Fertilitate non cedunt, opimamque
Messem serius tantum, sed non
minus percoquunt Sub his per
latus omne Vineæ porriguntur, u-
namque Faciem longè latèque
contexunt· quarum à Fine, imoque quasi Margine, Arbusti nas-
cuntur. Prata inde, Campique
Campi, quos nonnisi ingentes Boves & fortissima Aratra perfringunt tantis Glebis tenacissimarum
Solum, cum primum proscentur,
assurgit, ut noro demum Sulco
perdometur Prata floridi & gemmea, Trifolium, aliisque Herbis,
teneras semper & molles, & quasi
novas alunt; cuncta enim perennibus Rivis nutriuntur Sed ubi
Aqua plurimum, Palus nulla,
quin devexa Terra quicquid Liquoris accepit, nec absorbuit, effundit in Tiberim Medios ille
Agros secat Navium patiens,
omnesque Fruges devehit in Urbem,

lofty ancient Woods; which give opportunity to frequent and various
sorts of Hunting From thence the
Under-woods descend with the Mountains intermixt with these are small
Hills, of a strong fat Soil, (and
where tho' sought, a Stone can scarcely be found) and which for Fruitfulness do not yield to the most level
Fields, their Harvest is indeed somewhat later, but not less Under these
Hills the Vineyards extend themselves
on every side, and together form one
long spacious View their Extremities and Bottoms, are bounded as it
were, by a Border of Shrubs below
these are Meadows and Fields The
Fields, such as require the largest
Oxen and strongest Ploughs the stiff
Soil, when first stirred, rising in such
clods, that it is not sufficiently broken
till it has been plow'd nine times The
Meadows are flowery and budding,
producing the Trefoil, and other
Herbs, fresh and as it were always
springing, as being nourished by ever-
flowing Rivulets But tho' there be
much, there is no standing Water;
because as the Ground lies sheltering,
whatever Water it receives, and does
not imbibe, it throws into the Tiber
This River divides the Land and
in Winter and Spring is navigable,
and

bem; Hyeme duntaxat, & Ve-
re: Æstate summittitur, immen-
sique Fluminis Nomen arenti Al-
veo deserit, Autumno resumit
Magnam capies Voluptatem, si
hunc Regionis Situm ex Monte
prospexeris; neque enim Terras
tibi, sed Formam aliquam ad ex-
imiam Pulchritudinem pictam vi-
deberis cernere: ea Varietate, et
Descriptione, quocunque inside-
rint Oculi, reficientur. Villa in
Colle imo sita prospicit quasi ex
summo, ita leviter & sensim Clivo
fallente consurgit, ut cum ascendere
te non putes, sentias ascendisse. A
tergo Apenninum sed longius habet accipit ab hoc Auras quam-
libet sereno & placido Die, non
tamen acres & immodicas, sed
Spatio ipso lassas & infractas Magna sui Parte Meridiem spectat,
æstivumque Solem ab Hora sexta,
Hybernum aliquanto maturius, quasi invitat in Porticum latam, &
pro modo longam. Multa in hac
Membra; [1] Atrium etiam ex more
Veterum

and conveys the Provision of the Country to Rome; but in Summer, in a
dried up Chanel loses the Name of a
great River, which yet it resumes in
Autumn. You would take great Delight, in viewing the Country from
the top of a Mountain, for it would
not appear as real Land, but as an
exquisite Painting; there is that Variety of Landskip wheresoever you
cast your Eye. My Villa is placed
near the bottom of an Hill, but has
the same Prospect as from the top,
one is deceived in the Rise by its being
so gradual and easy, so that tho' you
don't perceive you ascend, you will find
you have. On the back but at a distance
are the Apennines; from whence in
the calmest Day, it receives Fresh, tho'
no sharp and immoderate Airs, the
Strength and Violence of which are
broken by the Distance from which they
come. The greatest Part of the House
is turn'd to the South, and in the
Summer from the sixth Hour, but in
the Winter somewhat sooner, does as
it were invite the Sun into a spacious
well-proportioned Porticus. In which
are several Parts; and an [1] Atrium
after

---

[1] *Atrium ex more Veterum*] To distinguish this from the *Atrium*, or Fore-court of *Laurentinum*,
Pliny gives us to understand, that this was a Building in the *Porticus*, and Part of the House it self,
and by what he says of its being after the manner of the Ancients, it may be supposed he speaks of
one of those *Atria* Described by *Vitruvius*

Veterum. Anté Porticum Xyſtus conciſus in plurimas·Species, diſtinctuſque Buxo; demiſſus inde, pronuſque Pulvinus, cui Beſtiarum Effigies invicem adverſas Buxus inſcripſit: ¹ Acanthus in Plano mollis, & pene dixerim liquidus. Ambit hunc ³ Ambulatio, preſſis varièque tonſis Viridibus incluſa: ab his Geſtatio in modum ⁴ Circi, quæ Buxum multiformem, humileſque & retentas manu Arbuſculas circumit: omnia Maceria muniuntur, hanc gradata Buxus operit & abſcondit Pratum inde non minus Natura, quam ſuperiora illa, Arte viſendum: Campi deinde, porro multaque alia Prati & Arbuſta. A Capite Porticûs Triclinium excurrit, Valvis Xyſtum deſinentem, & protinus Pratum, mul-

after the antient manner Before the Porticus is a Xyſtus cut in ſeveral Forms, and divided by Box; deſcending thence is a ſteep Slope, on which are the Forms of Beaſts fronting the oppoſite Box On the Flat grows the ſoft, and I had almoſt ſaid liquid ² Acanthus. This is ſurrounded by an ³ Ambulatio, which is encloſed by Greens cut in various Forms after this is a Geſtatio in the form of a ⁴ Circus, which encloſes the many-ſhaped Box, and Dwarf-trees that are rendered ſo by Art· the Whole is fenced in by a Wall, which is overcaſt and hid by ſeveral degrees of Box. From thence you have the View of a Meadow not leſs beautiful by Nature, than theſe the fore-mentioned Works of Art then you ſee Fields, with many other Meadows and Shrubs. from the Head of the Porticus a Triclinium runs out, from whoſe Folding-Doors you have juſt a View of the Xyſtus, and at a diſtance that of

Y   the

---

2. *Acanthus*.) Of this Plant there were two ſorts called by that Name, one of which had a very large Leaf, but the other, which was called *Mollis Acanthus*, was that with which they covered their Walks inſtead of *Turfs*, which we uſe at preſent

3. *Ambulatio*.) *Vitruvius* Lib. 5. Cap. 9. Speaks of theſe Walks or Places of Exerciſe that they had near their Theatres, and informs us that they were bounded by Greens, and not covered over Head by other Trees. To this walk he alſo gives the *Epithet* of *Hypethra* as he does afterwards to the *Xyſtus*, but that they were not the ſame, appears by this Ep. of *Pliny*, their difference being, that one, viz. the *Xyſtus* was open, not only over Head, but on the Sides, and the other had its bounds of Ever-Greens

4. *Circi*) Theſe were Places chiefly uſed for Publick Chariot-Races in *Rome*, the Form may be ſeen in moſt Authors that have wrote on the *Roman* Antiquities.

maltumque Ruris videt Feneftris: hinc Latus Xyfti & quod profilit Villæ, ac adjacentis Hippodromi Nemus Comifque profpectat Contra medium fere Porticum Diæta Paulum recedit, cingit Areolam, quæ quatuor Platanis inumbiatur: Inter has marmorco Labro Aqua exundat, circumjectafque Platanos, & fubjecta Platanis leni Afpergine fovet Eft in hac Diæta dormitorium Cubiculum, quod Diem, Clamorem, fonumque excludit junctaque quotidiana amicorum Cœnatio Areolam illam Porticus alia, eademque omnia, quæ Porticus afpicit Eft & aliud Cubiculum a proxima Platano, viride & umbrofum, Marmore exfculptum [6] Podio tenus: nec cedit Gratiæ

the Meadows, but from the Windows a large Profpect of the Country this way you behold one fide of the Xyftus, the Jettings-out of the Villa, and the fhady Wood of the adjacent Hippodrome. Oppofite almoft to the middle of the Porticus a Diæta feems a little to retire, and furrounds a fmall Area, that is fhaded by four Plane Trees Between thefe the Water flows from a marble [5] Bafon, and by its gentle Sprinkling nourifhes both the Planes and what grows under them In this Diæta is my Dormitorium Cubiculum, from whence the Light and all manner of Noife is excluded adjoining to it is my conftant private Cœnatio Another Porticus has alfo a view of this little Area, and every thing elfe with the former There is alfo another Cubiculum clofe to the firft Plane-tree, which makes it very fhady, this is adorned with Marble as high as its [6] Podium:

---

5 *Labium*] This Bowl or Part of the Fountain, was fo called from having its Edges made rounding and turning down, like the lower Lip of a Man

6 *Podium* By *Vitruvius*, feems to be a Pedeftal continued the whole length of a Building, and

a *Stylobata*
b *Podium*

is fo called both when there were Pillars placed on it, or only fupported a Wall When Pillars were
placed

Gratiæ Marmoris, Ramos, infidentefque Ramis Aves imitati Pictura; cui fubeft Fonticulus, in hoc Fonte Crater, circa Siphunculi plures mifcent jucundiffimum Murmur. In Cornu Porticus ampliffimum Cubiculum a Triclinio occurrit aliis Feneftris Xyftum, aliis defpicit Pratum, fed ante 7 Pifcinam, quæ Feneftris fervit ac fubjacet, Strepitu Vifuque jacunda· nam ex Edito defiliens Aqua, fufcepta Marmore albefcit Idem Cubiculum Hyeme tepidiffimum, quia plurimo fole perfunditur. Cohæret Hypocauftum, & fi Dies nubilus, immiffo Vapore, Solis vicem fupplet Inde Apodyterium Balnei laxum & hilare, excipit Cella frigidaria, in qua Baptifterium amplum atque opacum; fi natare latius aut tepidius

Podium· nor does a painting of Birds fitting on Trees, or even the Trees, fall fhort in Beauty of the Marble it felf; beneath this is a fmall Fountain, with a Bafon, round which the playing of feveral fmall Pipes makes a moft agreeable Murmuring In the corner of the Porticus coming from the Triclinium a very fpacious Cubiculum offers it felf Some of the Windows look on the Xyftus, and others on the Meadow, but thofe in the Front on a large 7 Pifcina, which lies under them and Delights both to the Ear and Eye for the Water falling from on high, is received in the Bafon and becomes white with Foam This Cubiculum is exceeding warm in Winter, as it has a great deal of Sun Joined to it is an Hypocauftum, fo that when the Weather is cloudy, by admitting its Heat, you may fupply the Want of the Sun After this, and a fpacious pleafant Apodyterium to the Baths, is the Cella Frigidaria, in which is a large dark Baptifterium; but if you are inclined to fwim more at

placed on the Sides of Buildings, fometimes inftead of having the Podium continue the whole Length in one Line, it was made to break forward under every Pillar, which Part fo advancing was called the *Stylobata*, and that which was betwixt the Pillars under the Wall was the *Podium*

By this paffage of *Pliny*, it appears that the *Podium* was ufed within Doors round the Walls of their Rooms

7 *Pifcina*] This word here fignifies the Bafon of a Fountain.

pid us velis, in Area Piſcina eſt, in proximo Puteus, ex quo poſſis rurſus aſtringi, ſi pœniteat Teporis Frigidariæ Cellæ connectitur media, cui ſol benigniſſime præſto eſt, caldariæ magis; prominet enim; in hac tres Deſcenſiones, duæ in Sole, tertia à Sole longius, à Luce non longius. Apodyterio ſuperpoſitum eſt Sphæriſterium, quod plura genera Exercitationis, plureſque Circulos capit Nec procul a Balineo Scalæ, quæ in Cryptoporticum ferunt, prius ad Diætas tres; harum alia Areolæ illi, in qua Platani quatuor, alia Prato, alia Vineis imminet diverſaſque Cœli Partes, ac Proſpectus habet In ſumma Cryptoporticu Cubiculum, ex ipſa Cryptoporticu exciſum, quod Hippodromum, Vineas, Montes intuetui Jungitur Cubiculum obvium Soli maxime hyberno. Hinc oritur Diæta, quæ Villæ Hippodromum

at large or warm, in the Area *is a* Piſcina, *and near it a Conveyance of Water, from whence you may again cloſe the Pores, when you think the Heat too great. To the* Cella Frigidaria *adjoins a middle one, to which the Sun is very liberally preſent, but is more ſo to the* Cella Caldaria; *becauſe it extends out further· In this are three Diviſions of ſeveral Degrees of Heat, two of which are expoſed to the Sun, the third tho' farther from its Heat, is not ſo from its Light. Over the* Apodyterium *is the* Sphæriſterium, *which contains Conveniencies for ſeveral ſorts of Exerciſe Not far from the Bath are Stairs that lead to the* Cryptoporticus, *after you have paſſed three Diætæ; one of which looks into the little Area, with Plane-trees, another to the Meadows, and the other has a Proſpect of the Vineyards, and ſeveral other Parts of the Country At the top of the* Cryptoporticus *is a* Cubiculum, *cut off from the very* Cryptoporticus, *which has a Proſpect of the* Hippodrome, Vineyards *and Mountains Joining to this is a* Cubiculum *that is much expoſed to the Sun in Winter. Here begins the* Diæta *that joins the* Villa *to the* Hippodrome*

diomum adnectit. Hæc Facies, hic Visus a Fronte : a Latere, æstiva Cryptoporticus in edito posita, quæ non aspicere Vineas, sed tangere videtur In media Triclinium saluberrimum afflatum ex Apenninis Vallibus recipit · post latissimis Fenestris vineas, Valvis æque Vineas, sed per Cryptoporticum quasi admittit: à Latere Triclinii, quod Fenestris caret, Scalæ Convivio utilia secretiore Ambitu suggerunt In Fine Cubiculum, cui non minus jucundum Prospectum Cryptoporticus ipsa, quam Vineæ præbent Subest Cryptoporticus subterraneæ similis, Æstate incluso Frigore riget; contentaque Acre suo nec desiderat Auras nec admittit. Post utramque Cryptoporticum, unde Triclinium definit, incipit Porticus· ante medium Diem, hyberna; inclinato die, æstiva · hac adeuntur Diætæ duæ, quarum in altera Cubicula quatuor, altera tria, ut circuit Sol, aut

podrome *This is the Form and Prospect it has on the Front on the Side, this Summer* Cryptoporticus *being placed aloft, does not only see, but seems to touch the Vineyards In the middle is a* Triclinium *that receives most healthy Air from the Valleys of the* Apennines: *From behind, the large Windows have a Prospect of the Vineyards, as have also the Folding-Doors, but that as it were through the* Cryptoporticus: *On the side of the* Triclinium, *that has no Windows is a winding Staircase, that affords a more private Passage for what may be requisite at private Entertainments At the end of it is a* Cubiculum *that has not a less pleasant Prospect of the* Cryptoporticus, *than of the Vineyards Under it is a* Cryptoporticus *built like a Vault, which by being shut close is cold in Summer ; and contented with its own Airs, neither admits nor requires any other After you have pass'd both* Cryptoporticus, *where the* Triclinium *ends, begins a* Porticus: *which before Noon, is cold; but warm, towards the Close of the Day To this are joyn'd two* Diætæ, *one of which contains four, and the other three* Cubicula; *these as the*

Z   *Sun*

aut Sole utuntur, aut Umbra. Hanc Difpofitionem, Amœnita- temque Tectorum longe præcedit ⁸ Hippodromus; medius patefcit, ftatimque intrantium Oculis to- tus offertur· Platanis circuitur, illæ Hedera veftiuntur, utque fum- mæ fuis, ita imæ alienis Frondi- bus virent: Hedera Truncum & Ramos pererrat, vicinafque Pla- tanos Tranfitu fuo copulat: has Buxus interjacet; exteriores Buxos circumvenit Laurus, Umbræque Platanorum fuam confert. Rectus hic Hippodromi Limes in extre- ma Parte Hemicyclo frangitur, mutatque Faciem; Cupreffis am- bitur, & tegitur, denfiore Umbra opicior, nigriorque interioribus Circulis (funt enim plures) pu- riffimum Diem recipit, indé eti- am Rofas offert, Umbrarumque Frigus non ingrato Sole diftin- guit. Finito vario illo, multipli- cique

Sun goes round, are ufed either as that, or Shade is requifite This Dif- pofition, and Delightfulnefs of the Houfe is far excelled by that of the ⁸ Hippodrome it is open in the Mid- dle, and prefents it felf at once to the Eyes of thofe that enter it It is fur- rounded with Plane-Trees, which are cover'd with Ivy, and as the Tops are with their own, the Bottoms are green with foreign Leaves. the Ivy runs ftragling over the Trunks and Branches, and in its Paffage joyns together the neighbouring Plane- Trees between which are Box-Trees; the outermoft of which are encom- paffed with Lawrel, which affifts the Plane-Trees in caufing a Shade. The ftraight Bounds of the Hippodrome at the further End being broken in- to a Semicircle, change their Form, and are fhaded and furrounded with Cyprefs-Trees, which give a darker, and blacker Caft to the Place yet in the innermoft Circles (for there are feveral) it receives a moft clear Light, and is for that Reafon productive of Rofes, fo that the coolnefs of the Shade is agreeably mixt with the Pleafures of the Sun Having finifh'd this courfe, by

---

⁸ *Hippodromus*] As the *Circi* were in *Rome,* fo in feveral *Grecian* Cities this was the Place for Horfe Races By the Account we have of the *Hippodromus,* it feems in all Refpects to have been like the *Circus,* except that inftead of having Seats all round, it was furrounded by a *Porticus*

cique Curvamine, recto Limiti redditur, nec huic uni; nam Viæ plures intercedentibus Buxis dividuntur. Alibi Pratulum, alibi ipfa Buxus intervenit in Formas mille defcripta; Literis interdum, quæ modo Nomen Domini dicunt, modo Artificis: alternis Metulæ furgunt, alternis inferta funt Poma: & in Opere urbaniffimo, fubita velut illati Ruris Imitatio, medium in Spatium brevioribus utrinque Platanis adornatur. Poft has, Acanthus hinc inde lubricus & flexuofus, deinde plures Figuræ, pluraque Nomina In Capite 9 Stibadium candido Marmore, Vite protegitur; Vitem quatuor Columellæ Caryftiæ fubeunt: e Stibadio Aqua, velut expreffa cubantium Pondere, Sipunculis effluit, cavato Lapide fufcipitur, gracili Marmore continetur, atque ita occulte temperatur, ut impleat, nec redundet. 10 Guftatorium

by many and various Windings, it returns again to the ftraight Bounds of the Hippodrome, yet not the fame way; for there are many Paths divided from one another by Rows of Box In one Place is a little Meadow, in another the Box defcribes a thoufand different Forms; fometimes in Letters which tell the Name of the Mafter, fometimes that of the Artificer in fome Places they grow like Cones, and in other Globular and after a moft elegant Tafte, a fudden Imitation of the Country feems accidentally introduced in the Middle, and is adorned on each Side with fhort Plane-Trees Behind thefe, is a Wall of the flippery winding Acanthus; and then more Figures, and more Names At the head of this is a 9 Stibadium of white Marble, covered with Vines, which are fupported by four Pillars of Caryftian Marble Out of the Stibadium, the Water flows from feveral fmall Pipes, as if preffed out by the Weight of what lies on it, and is receiv'd and contained in a Bafon, fo artfully order'd, that tho full, it does not run over The 10 Guftatorium

9. *Stibadium*.) Signified originally a fixed Seat, or Bed of Earth, covered with Grafs or Boughs, which Name, as by this Paffage appears, was afterwards given to thofe that were made of Marble Their Ufe was to lie on when they eat abroad in their Gardens

10 *Guftatorium*) It was the Cuftom of the *Romans* to eat but two Meals in the Day, the firft of

rium graviorque Cœnatio Margini imponitur, levior Navicularum & Avium Figuris Innatans circuit Contra Fonsegerit Aquam & recipit, nam expulsa in Altum in se cadit, junctisque Hiatibus & absorbetur & tollitur E Regione Stibadii adversum Cubiculum tantum Stibadio reddit Ornatus, quantum accipit ab illo. a Marmore splendet, Valvis in Viridia prominet, & exit: alia Viridia superioribus inferioribusque Fenestris suspicit, despicitque Mox Zothecula refugit quasi in Cubiculum idem atque aliud, Lectulus hic & undique Fenestræ, & tamen Lumen obscurum Umbra premente nam lætissima Vitis per omne Tectum in Culmen nititur & ascendit Non secus ibi, quam in Nemore jaces, Imbrem tantum tanquam in Nemore non sentias.

hic

tatorium, *and heavier sorts of Cœnatio are plac'd on the Margin, but the lighter swim about in the Form of small Ships and Birds Over against the* Stibadium *is a Fountain that casts forth and receives Water, which being play'd up to a great height falls into it again, and runs off through Drains that are join'd to it Opposite to the* Stibadium *is a* Cubiculum, *which returns as great Grace to the* Stibadium *as it receives from it. Splendid it is with Marble, its Folding-Doors jutt out and open into Places fill'd with Greens, and has different Prospects of other Greens both from upper and lower Windows beyond this a* Zothecula *flies back, and is as it were the same* Cubiculum *with this as well as another, and has in it a Bed, and Windows on every Side, yet still has a dim Light occasion'd by the Shade for a very beautiful Vine climbs up and covers the whole Building to the Top Nor do you lie otherwise here, than in a Wood ; only you are not so sensible of Rains as you would*

---

of which they took very sparingly, and only as it were tasted of their Victuals, from whence it was called *Gustatorium*, and the latter, which was after Mid day, was called the *Cæna*, and from these two Meals, those Dishes on which the Meat was served up at each, took their Names ; the *Gustatorium*, by *Pliny's* Account of it, seems to have been larger than those Dishes called *Cœnationes*, and might probably have been so, because at that Repast all the several things of which they eat were brought in at once, but the other Vessels which were for their greater Meal were changed at every Course

hic quoque Fons nafcitur, fimul-
que fubducitur　Sunt Locis pluribus difpofita Sedilia è Marmore,
quæ Ambulatione feffos, ut Cubiculum ipfum juvant: Fonticuli
Sedilibus adjacent, per totum Hippodromum inductis Fiftulis ftre-
punt Rivi, & qua Manus duxit,
fequuntur　His nunc illa Viridia,
nunc hæc, interdum fimul omnia
lavantur　Vitaffem jamdudum, ne
viderer argutior, nifi propofuiffem omnes Angulos tecum Epiftola circumire　Neque enim ve-
rebar, ne laboriofum effet legenti
tibi, quod vifenti non fuiffet·
præfertim cum interquiefcere fi
liberet, de pofitaque Epiftola,
quafi refidere fæpius poffes. Præterea indulfi Amori meo; amo
enim, quæ maxima ex Parte ipfe
inchoavi, aut inchoata percolui.
In fumma (cur enim non aperi-
am tibi vel Judicium meum vel
Errorem?) primum ego Officium
Scriptoris exiftimo, ut Titulum
　　　　　　　　　　　　　　fuum

wou'd be there　here alfo a Fountain
fprings up and prefently difappears
Difpofed in feveral Places are marble Seats, to eafe thofe that are tired
with walking, as well as the Cubiculum itfelf　Near to thefe Seats
are fmall Fountains, while gentle
Streams brought in by Pipes run
murmuring thro the whole Hippodrome, and flow wherefoever the hand
directs; and from them fometimes
Thefe, fometime Thofe, and at other
times all the Greens are watered together　I had fooner taken care to
avoid being thought talkative, if I
had not propofed in my Epiftle to
carry you round to every minute
Part of my Villa. Nor could I ap-
prehend it would be any Trouble for
you to read, what would not be fo
to fee　and the more, becaufe whenever weary of reading, you might at
any time fit down, as it were, and
reft yourfelf, by laying afide the Epiftle　Befides, I have indulged my own
Paffion; for I take great Delight in
what I have either begun, or finifhed
after it was begun　In fine (for why
fhou'd I not fubmit to you my Opinion, or perhaps Miftakes?) I think
the firft thing an Author fhould do,
is to read over his Title Page, and

　　　　A a　　　　　　　　　　　at

suum legat, atque indentidem in-
terroget se, quid cœperit scribere:
sciatque, si Materiæ immoratur,
non esse longum: longissimum, si
aliquid accersit atque attrahit
Vides, quot versibus Homerus,
quot Virgilius Arma, hic Æneæ,
Achillis ille, describat: brevis tamen uterque est, quia facit quod
instituit Vides, ut Aratus minu-
tissima etiam Sidera consectetur &
colligat, modum tamen servat Non
enim Excursus hic ejus, sed Opus
ipsum est. Similiter nos, ut parva
magnis conferamus, cum totam Villam Occulis tuis subjicere cona-
mur, si nihil inductum & quasi
devium loquimur, non Epistola,
quæ describit, sed Villa, quæ de-
scribitur magna est. Verum illuc, unde cœpi; ne secundum
Legem meam Jure reprehendar,
si longior fuero in hoc, quod ex-
cessi Habes Causas, cur ego Thufcos meos Thusculanis, Tyburtinis,
Præneftinifque meis præponam
Nam super illa, quæ retuli, altius
ibi Otium, & pinguius, eoque fe-
curius, nulla necessitas Togæ, Nemo
accer-

at the same time examine himself
what it was he proposed to write
he may then be sensible, that where-
ever he may have dwelt upon material Circumstances, he has not been
prolix, but extremely tedious where-
ever he has introduced any thing
far-fetch'd or foreign to the Subject
You see, in how many Verses Homer
describes the Arms of Achilles, and
Virgil those of Æneas: yet both are
concise, because themselves invented
what they described You see also
how Aratus searches after and reckons up the minutest Stars, yet is not
tedious; for his is not properly a
Digression, but the Work it self.
Thus, if we may compare small things
with great, while I endeavour to
bring the whole Villa before your
Eyes, if I treat of nothing forced or
from the Purpose, it is not the Epiftle, but the described Villa that is
large. But to return to where I left
off; left I offend against mine own
Rule, if I should be longer in this
Digression You have here the Reasons why I prefer my Villa of Tufcum to those of Tusculum, Tyber
and Præneste But besides these
which I have related, I there enjoy
a more profound, easy, and secure
Retirement; there is no Occasion for
the

accerſitor ex proximo; placida omnia & Quieſcentia, quod ipſum Salubritate Regionis, ut purius Cœlum ut Aer liquidior accedit: ibi Animo, ibi Corpore maxime valeo. Nam ſtudiis Animum, venatu Corpus exerceo. Mei quoque nuſquam ſalubrius degunt, uſque adhuc certe Neminem ex iis, quos eduxeram mecum (venia ſit dicto) ibi amiſi. Dii modo in poſterum, hoc mihi Gaudium, hanc Gloriam Loco ſervent Vale

the Gown, nor am I troubled with Viſitors; all things are pleaſant and quiet, which adds to the Health of the Place, as much as the pure and ſerene Air I there enjoy a perfect Health of Mind and Body, for I exerciſe my Mind with Study, and my Body with Hunting My Domeſticks alſo want not their Health as yet (pardon the Expreſſion) I have not loſt one of them I brought with me May the Gods for the time to come preſerve this Pleaſure to me, and Reputation to the Place. Farewel.

REMARKS

ON

TUSCUM.

THE Defcription of this *Villa*, as well as that of *Laurentinum*, *Pliny* has ranged under Three Heads, *viz.* *Temperiem Cœli*, *Regionis Situm*, & *Amœnitatem Villæ*. the two former of which wholly relating to the Situation, he has confidered them with refpect to Health, Conveniency, and Pleafure.

Cœlum eft Hyeme, &c] *Pliny* was in a particular Manner obliged to take Notice of the Healthinefs of the Situation, to defend his Judgment againft the Opinion of his Friend, who had imputed to him the Building in a bad Climate *Vitruvius*, Lib 1. Cap 4 fays, the Ancients ufed to fearch the Livers of Beafts that fed where they defigned to build; which if they found vitiated, they concluded bad Water and Pafturage was the Caufe, and that it would not fare better with thofe who fhould fettle there, whofe Diet muft be of thofe Beafts, and were obliged to partake of the fame Water· but here, as our Author was only chargedwith the Unwholefomenefs of the Place, as proceeding from another Caufe, *viz* bad Air, he was not obliged to fearch for fuch Proofs, and only endervours to fatisfy his Friend, that on the contrary the Health of the Place was wholly owing to the Goodnefs of the Air, and tho' cold and fiofty in Winter, yet to its temperate Breezes in Summer

B b   (the

(the time he refided there) he imputes the long Lives of the Inhabitants

Regionis Forma pulcherrima, &c] The Situation with refpect to the
Country it felf, is here confidered under three Views *viz* its Pleafures,
its Fertility, and the Conveniency of the navigable River   The Reafon, that in this Epiftle he takes no Notice of the Neighbourhood of
Tifernum, as he does of *Oftia* in the former, and that he is not fo
particular in mentioning feveral other things he fpeaks of in the Situation of *Laurentinum,* was becaufe he here defcribed a *Villa* on a large
Eftate, where, as it has been before obferved, it may be taken for gran-
ted he had within himfelf all Neceffaries of Life   The Defcription
he gives of the Face of this Country, fhews there was nothing wanting to make the Profpect delightful, there being fuch an agreeable
Mixture of Highwoods, Hills covered with Corn, Underwoods, Vineyards, Shrubs, Fields, Meadows, and Water   Befides the Pleafures of
this Country to the Eye, there was another the Woods afforded,
which was a Supply of feveral forts of Game for Chafe, which he was
the more induced to take Notice of here, becaufe it was a Diverfion
he extremely delighted in, as may be collected from feveral of his
Epiftles   By his Account of the Face of this Country, it would feem as
if he had no other Defign but to defcribe its Beauties, but if further
examined, it will be found that it alfo was laid out according to the
niceft Rules of Agriculture, and that it contained almoft all thofe
Products which the Writers on that Science efteemed effential to a
compleat Farm; and which *Cato,* Cap 1*ft,* divides into nine Branches,
*viz Vinea, Hortus irriguus, Salictum, Oletum, Pratum, Campus fru-
mentarius, Sylva cœdua, Arbuftum & Glandaria Sylva* fix of which,
viz the two firft and four laft are mentioned here, and it is not to be
fuppofed but the *Salictum* and *Hortus irriguus* were there alfo, fince
the Ground was fo proper for them, that the *Oletum* only was wanting, of which in the former part of this Epiftle he fays the Climate
would not admit   The Principal of thefe were difpofed by the fkilful

Huf-

Husbandman, as the Product required more or lefs Heat, for which
Varro, Lib. 1. Cap 7 gives thefe Directions: On the higheft Lands,
which being the coldeft, were moft unfit for Tillage, he orders the
Woods to be planted, and the Vines lower down the Hills, which
in that Climate he thought beft to be in a moderate Heat, and the
Corn which required the ftrongeft, to be fowed in the Fields that
lay in the Plains; which was the Reafon why *Pliny,* in this Defcription takes Notice, that tho' fome of the Corn-Fields near him were
on the Hills, yet they were as fruitful as thofe in the Plain, tho'
the Corn was not fo foon ripe   This is the only Paffage where this
Defcription fwerves from the fore-mentioned Rules; and tho' fome of
the Corn-Fields were on the Hills, the greater Part were more properly in the Plain

Campi quos nonnifi ingentes, &c] That thefe Lands were fertile may
be concluded from the Account he gives of the Strength of the
Soil; and it is well worth noting their extraordinary Diligence in pre-
paring their Land by plowing it nine Times; which that it was cufto-
mary in thofe Parts, may be likewife proved from *Pliny* the Naturalift,
Lib. 1. Cap 5 *Spiffius Solum plerumque in Italia quinto Sulco feri me-
lius eft in Thufcis vero nono*

Prata florida & Gemmea, &c] By the Character of thefe Meadows
it appears they had all Advantages requifite to make them fit for Pafturage, and pleafant to the Sight; to which the conftant Rivulets
very much contributed, as they alfo did to the Health of the Situation, which might not have been fo great, had the Place abounded
with ftanding Water

Medios ille Agros, &c] As the real Face of thefe Lands did in all
other Refpects anfwer that which *Columella,* Lib. 1 Cap 7. defcribes,
and fays was only to be wifh'd for; fo neither did it want the Conveniency of a navigable River, which in the fame Author is mentioned as

a material Advantage to a Situation The Dryness of this River in Summer was no great Loss to the Husbandman, since it appears that the Country was sufficiently supplied with Water for Use, and the Navigation of the River was not wanted till the Harvest was got in, at which Time (as is here observed) it again resumed its Course, so that they could then send their Corn, Wine, &c. by Water to *Rome*; and it is likely this was the Cause he takes no Notice of the Roads about this *Villa* besides the Conveniencies of this River, when it was filled with Water, it was no small Addition to the Beauty of the Valley.

Magnam capies Voluptatem, &c] The Description of this Country seems to have been drawn from the Place the House stood upon, or something higher, from whence, as he observes, the Whole must appear like one entire beautiful Landskip, the Distance allowing an Opportunity of seeing all those Parts at one View, which he has before described distinctly.

Villa in Colle imo sita, &c] From the Form of the Country he proceeds to take Notice of the Place on which the House was seated, which was exactly conformable to the Rules laid down by those who have given Directions for the Situation of a *Villa* like This, who, as has been observed in the former Part of this Work for several Reasons condemn the placing a House on the Top of a Hill, or in the Bottom of a Valley, the middle Site being most commodious and secure, as this appears to have been: by which Means, it was not only freed from the Inconveniencies, to which other Situations are subject, but had also the Benefit of receiving the cool Airs from the *Apennines,* which was a singular Advantage to this Summer *Villa,* that was not placed so low, but it could command a Prospect of the whole Country, nor so high, as not to have Water in several Parts of the Garden, which it is probable was collected from Springs in the neighbouring Hills, and conveyed thither by an Aqueduct

Magni

*Magna fui Parte Meridiem fpectat æftivumque Solem ab Hora fexta,
hybernum aliquanto maturius,* &c.] *Vitruvius,* Lib 6 Cap. 1. fays thus:
In Northern Countries, Houfes fhould have high Roofs, be much enclofed, not have many Apertures, and turned to the warm Quarters
of the Heavens: but on the contrary, in the Regions of the *South,*
where they fuffer through too much Heat, Houfes fhould be made
more open, and turned to the *North* or *North Eaft*; fo that what is
hurtful through natural Caufes, may be corrected by Art This
Rule, which doubtlefs was carefully obferved by the Architects of his
Time, feems but in part to be followed by the Defigner of thefe *Villas*
of *Pliny*; for tho' he has made this Summer *Villa* more open than the
other, yet it appears at firft Sight as if he no ways regarded the Rule
of placing the Houfe, as the Seafon it was built for required · but if
examined into it will be found, that tho' the Front of his Winter
Villa was placed to the *North,* and that of his Summer which required
to be cool, to the *South*; yet thofe Fronts ferved moftly for the inferiour Conveniencies of the Houfes, and to guard the principal Parts in each
Villa from what was moft troublefome In order the better to underftand
the true Difpofition of the Front of this Houfe, it may not be amifs
to examine the Method obferved by the *Romans* in the Meafure of the
Day; which by *Palladius* appears in his Time to have been divided
into Eleven Parts; fo that there were Five Hours both before and after
the fixth, or middle Hour of the Day. Their Divifions in the Time
of *Auguftus* were marked by the Shade of an Obelisk, that was placed
by his Order in the *Campus Martius,* and which the Elder *Pliny* fays,
was an hundred and fixteen Feet and nine Inches long. The Method
of making thefe Sun-dials is defcribed at large by *Vitruvius,* Lib 9.
Cap 8 but thefe were only of Ufe in clear Days, and till the Five Hundred ninety fifth Year of the City, as the fame *Pliny* tells us, Lib. 7
Cap. 60. they had not perfected an Invention to meafure the Hours
without the Help of the Sun: Thefe *Horologia* feem to have meafured
the whole Space of Time from Sun-rifing to Sun-rifing, into as many
equal Parts as was thought proper; by which Means, the fixth Hour of

C c

the

the Day, except at the Time of the *Æquinox*, never happened when the Sun was full *South*, it being in Summer before that time, and in Winter after; so that during the Winter the greater Part of the Day was before the sixth Hour, and in Summer after: and it seems as if the Measure of Time which our Author followed was according to this Rule, otherwise it would be very difficult to reconcile what he says in this Passage to Reason. What has been here observed, may serve to prove that this House did not face full *South*, but was rather turned as *Palladius* Lib 1 Tit 8 directs, where he says, the whole Length of the Front should be so disposed as to receive at one Angle the Winter's rising Sun, and turn a little from its setting; by these Means it will admit the Light of the Sun in Winter, and be insensible of its Heat in Summer: which Rule seems to be founded on the same Motives that guided *Pliny* in the placing his House.

Porticum latam, &c] That they had no set Form for the Plans of their *Villas*, but varied them as Conveniency required, appears by these two *Villas* of *Pliny*, as also that as Pleasure or Necessity directed, they neglected to follow the Custom *Vitruvius*, Lib. 6. Cap 8. says was observed in his Time in building *Villas*, where he says, that in those for Pleasure, the first thing they entered was a *Peristyle*, then an *Atrium*, which had paved *Porticus's* about it that were turned towards the Walks and *Palæstra*, or Places of Exercise. The Length of Time betwixt *Vitruvius* and *Pliny* had so far altered Customs, that there seems to be but a small Resemblance of the more ancient Manner of Building in either of his *Villas*; and in this of *Tuscum*, the first thing that offers it self instead of the *Peristyle*, is the *Gestatio*, a Part never mentioned by *Vitruvius*; beyond which indeed, after having passed two other Places of Exercise, is the *Atrium*, adjoyning to which is a *Porticus*, and tho' not in the Manner *Vitruvius* directs, yet it is turned to the *Ambulatio* and *Xystus*, which was a Place of Exercise as well as the *Palæstra*. The *Porticus* here first mentioned, besides the Exercise of Walking, which was its proper Ufe, had this Conveniency, that by its Breadth it kept off the Heat of the Sun from all thofe Parts that opened into it, and looked *Southward*; befides which, it ferved as it were the better to joyn all thofe Members of the Houfe into one Body. It does not appear by any Paffage in *Vitruvius*, that the *Romans* had any Rule to govern them in the Proportion of their *Porticus's*, nor indeed was it neceffary that thofe Places, which in their Buildings were made very long for the Sake of Exercife only, fhould have a Breadth proportioned to their Length; and as this was defigned for that Ufe, it is likely he meant its Breadth and Length bore a feeming, rather than a real Proportion.

Atrium ex more Veterum, &c.] It has been before remarked that in the Manner of defigning this *Villa*, the Method laid down by *Vitruvius* was in fome Degree obferved, and among other things, was the old-fafhioned *Atrium*; for the Difpofition of which *Vitruvius* gives Directions, Lib 6 Cap 4 as alfo for the Proportion of the *Tablinum* that was joined to it. This *Atrium*, probably one of the largeft Rooms in the Houfe, and not the worft adorned, he takes fo flight a Notice of, becaufe there was a ftanding Rule for the making of them; as alfo becaufe its Office was only for Clients, and thofe Servants called *Atrienfes* to wait in, and this and the *Porticus* feem to have been the only Parts of this *Villa* that were common for all to enter. After the Defcription of which, before he enters upon the more private Parts of the Houfe, he thought proper to mention thofe Works of Art that lay before the *Porticus*; the firft, or that which lay next it, was the *Xyftus*, beyond which was the *Ambulatio*

Xyftus concifus, &c] By his Character of this Place, it feems to have been deck'd up like the modern Parterres, and it was here that he tells us, *Lib.* 9 *Ep* 36. he ufed to exercife himfelf in Walking, till the Sun or bad Weather obliged him to retire to the *Cryptoporticus*. By feveral Paffages in this Defcription it feems to have been not only in the Front, but alfo on the Sides of the Houfe; and it appears to

have

have been upon a Ground raifed higher than any other Part that lay before the *Villa,* which was an Advantage to the Houfe, to which it feemed to ferve for a Bafe, and raifed it out of all Inconveniencies of Wet, and gave it a more graceful View to thofe that faw it from the Bottom, than if it had ftood upon a Level with the Road or Entrance of the Avenue. The Slope, which defcended from the *Xyftus* to the *Geftatio,* lying upon a Line with the Eyes of thofe who came to the *Villa,* he thought proper to adorn with that fort of Trees, which might eafieft be cut into any Manner of Form.

Acanthus in Plano, &c] The Exercife of walking in the Sun, as already obferved in the Remarks on *Laurentinum,* was fometimes taken naked and barefoot, for which Reafon it was neceffary to make thofe Walks as foft as poffible; as this was planted with what he calls the *Acanthus*; of which there were two forts, in Imitation of the larger and rougher of which the antient *Corinthian* Capitals were adorned, and the other which he here fpeaks of feems by its Character to refemble Mofs

Ambit hunc Ambulatio, &c] The *Ambulatio* bounded the *Xyftus* after the Manner mention'd by *Vitruvius,* who in feveral Paffages places them near the Houfes of the moft principal *Romans,* and in *Lib 5 Cap* 9. he fpeaks of publick Ones in the City near their Theatres, which he there calls *hypethra Ambulationes,* and in the fame Place gives the Reafon for their being uncovered, as alfo for their being bounded with Ever-Greens as this was; the *Xyftus,* as well as the *Ambulatio,* was alfo an open Walk, but then it had no Trees or Hedges to bound its Sides, as the other had

Ab his Geftatio in Modum Circi, &c] Further from the Houfe, beyond the *Ambulatio,* lay this Place of Exercife, to which he chofe to give the Form of the *Circus,* becaufe the Exercifes that were ufed in it were like thofe that were ufed in thofe publick Places of Diverfion:
                                                                                                which

CORVS

FAVONIVS

a. Fertum
b. Atrium
c. Tablinum
d. Areola
e. Dormitorium estivalium
f. Cænatio
g. Fertum alia
h. Cubiculum
i. Cubiculum amplissimum
k. Hypotesium
l. Cella frigidaria
m. Cella media
n. Cella caldaria
o. Scala quæ in Crypto-
porticum ferunt
p. Porta quæ Villa Hip-
podromum adducit
q. Scala
r. Cryptoporticus subter-
ranea pensilis
s. Porticus ante medium s
t. Porta Dua

Cubiculum Subtily
Bramatis

AVSTER EVRONOTV

THRASCIAS   SEPTENTRIO

VULTURNUS

SOLANUS

Oriens Solstity Æstiv

a Faltnum
b Propnigeon
  Hypocauston
d Unctuarium
e Scala
f Bibliotheca
g Basilica
h Culina
i Carnarium
k Furnus
l Apothecarum
m Cellæ Servorum
n Prcaton

:h this not only refembled in Form, but in Ornaments ; with this
:rence only, that as the Ornaments of That were of Stone, thofe
his confifted of Trees cut in the fame Shapes, and this *Geftatio* was
ided with Degrees of Box, as the *Circus* with Seats of Stone for the
:lators : And as the middle Part of That was filled with Obelisks,
.rs, Pillars, and Arches, fo This was with Box-Trees and other
ibs, probably cut into the fame Forms ; which Imitation muft have
·ded an agreeable View to thofe, who paffed thro' this *Geftatio*,
feems to have been a fort of Avenue to the Houfe.

·*ratum inde*, &c] With the *Geftatio* ended the rifing Ground
·reon the Houfe ftood, at the Bottom of which lay the Meadows
Fields that have been fpoken of in the Situation, and are here
·n repeated, to fhew the agreeable Profpect that was enjoyed from
Porticus, and thofe other Parts already defcribed.

· *Capite Porticus Triclinium*, &c] Having done with the Avenue,
lks, and thofe Parts of the Houfe which were open to all, he comes
: to fpeak of thofe to which *Vitruvius* tells us Nobody had Accefs,
·pt the Invited ; the chief of thefe in all *Villas* was the *Triclinium*,
:h in both *Pliny*'s is the firft Member he takes Notice of. This
is to have had the Preference to the other Members that were
·ie *Porticus*, and was placed at the Head of it, and muft (as ap-
·s by other Parts of the Defcription) have been at the *Weft* End,
hat the Front of it faced *Eaftward* It has been obferved, that
·n all their Eating-Rooms they were defirous of having as pleafant
·ofpect as they could ; and as the beft and moft extenfive Profpect
·n this *Villa* lay *South* of it, in this Summer Eating-Room they
·ld not have fo conveniently enjoyed it without being incommoded
·Heat, had not this Room been made to advance out beyond the other
·ts of the Houfe, as upon feveral Accounts it appears to have done ;
·vhich Means at the fame time that it had an agreeable Profpect on
·h Sides, the Heat of the Sun was allay'd by the Breezes that he be-

fore obferved conftantly blew in the Summer from the *North*; and it does not appear to have had any opening *Wefterly*, where the Sun was oppofite to it at the time of their Eating in that Seafon. As *Pliny* has not told the Form of this *Triclinium*, and as *Vitruvius* has proved, that that built after the *Egyptian* Manner was moft proper to avoid the Heat, and at the fame time enjoy the Light of the Sun: in the Plan is drawn a *Triclinium* after that Manner, only with this Difference, that for the Sake of a Profpect, inftead of having the lower Part quite fhut up, there are here Doors and Windows which might have been fhut or opened at Pleafure. To the *Eaft* this *Triclinium* had only a View of the *Porticus*, but from its Sides enjoyed at once the two moft agreeable Profpects of the Country, which no one Room defcribed did befide this. On the *South* it had a Profpect of the *Area* of that natural *Amphitheatre* which has been defcribed, and *North-ward* were thofe Woods which covered the Tops of the Hills that bounded it

Contra mediam fere Porticum, &c] If there were no more Rooms in this *Diæta* than thofe here mentioned, they could not without the Affiftance of the *Porticus* and *Atrium* be well contrived to bound three Sides of this *Areola*, though it is likely there might have been more Rooms than the three that are named The *Procœton*, which was in moft Appartments, is not mentioned in any Part of this *Villa*, *Pliny* being not fo particular in this Defcription as in that of *Laurentinum*.

Eft in hac Diæta Dormitorium, &c] The following Rooms in this Defcription, as well as thofe Rooms that follow the *Triclinium* of the other *Villa*, feem to have been fet afide for the Mafter's proper Appartment; and *Pliny* no where elfe mentions *Dormitorium* or *Cubiculum noctis*, he only takes Notice, that this Chamber had the fame Qualifications with thofe that were in his Garden *Diæta* of *Laurentinum*, except the *Hypocaufton*, which this Summer Room did not want.

Junctaque

Junctaque quotidiana Amicorum Cœnatio.] This private Eating-Room, which in this Place only is mentioned as part of a *Diæta*, as well as the forementioned *Triclinium,* was conveniently placed for the Baths, from the Ufe of which they immediately came to it. Its Difpofition on the Side of this Court was very proper for Summer, being by the Buildings that furrounded the *Areola* fheltered from all Parts but the *North,* to which Point *Vitruvius* directs their Summer Eating-Rooms to be turned, it being fo placed as to have no other Benefit from the *North,* but its cool Airs; the Juttings out of the Building taking off all other Profpects, there is no mention made of any but the *Areola,* whofe Ornaments feem to have been the principal One it had This *Cœnatio* was called *quotidiana Amicorum,* to diftin-guifh it from the *Triclinium,* that in *Lib.* i. *Ep* 3. he ftiles *populare,* where larger Entertainments were made for many Guefts, and not fo conftantly ufed.

Areolam illam Porticus alia, &c] This *Porticus* ftanding *North* and *South* as in the Plan, muft have been a conftant cool Place for walk-ing in, when the greater *Porticus* which flanked to the *South,* may have been too warm. And it is probable its Difpofition was the fame as the others; and fince it is faid to have the fame Profpect with the greater *Porticus,* it muft have opened into it, otherwife it could not have anfwered that and other Parts of the Defcription The Advantages of this leffer *Porticus* were feveral, as it ferved for a Paffage to the *Areola,* and to the Stairs that were by the Bath, and fupported one of the three *Diæta* that furrounded the Court above Stairs

Eft & aliud Cubiculum, &c] The *Areola,* which by its Fountain, Verdure, and Shades, afforded an agreeable Refrefhment to all the Rooms on the Ground Floor that looked into it, muft have been in a more particular Manner beneficial to this *Cubiculum,* which feems to have been a Room for Day Sleep, and made as cool as Art and

the

the Place could admit of; and to make it the more fo, befides the Fountain that was without, there was alfo another within, whofe murmuring Noife added to the Pleafure of the Room This is the only Room in either *Villa*, of whofe Ornaments he has given any Account, and this was adorned according to the niceft Judgment The *Podium*, which has been explained in the Notes on this Epiftle, if the Height of the Room allowed of it, reached as high as the Bottom of the Windows, which being on a Ground Floor, and made damp by the Fountain that was in it, the Plaiftering muft have been damaged, had it been continued down to the Pavement; to remedy which it was encrufted fo high with Marble, from whence to the Ceiling it was probably cover'd with Stucco, as the Rooms of the Antients moftly were, whofe Sides they defigned to paint, for Reafons, as *Vitruvius, Lib 7 Cap 3* gives us in thefe Words, *Colours well laid upon wet Plaifter don't fade, but continue frefh for ever* The fame Author, who thought it neceffary that an Architect fhould be a Judge of thofe other Arts, with which Architecture ufed to be adorned, in the 5th Chap of the fame Book, has ventured to pafs a Cenfure upon thofe Painters of his Time, who were addicted to what at prefent are called *Gothick* Ornaments, condemning all Imitations that do not refemble the Truth, or at leaft the Verifimilitude; and in the fame Place feems to hint as if there were particular Paintings proper to particular Rooms. *Pliny*, who in feveral of his Epiftles proves himfelf an excellent Judge in this Art, has made choice of the moft fimple and natural Manner of defigning to adorn this Room; preferring here that Manner which only pleafed the Eye by Colours, to that which moved the Paffions, as Hiftory Pieces, which perhaps he thought more proper for larger and more publick Rooms, fuch as the *Atrium, Triclinium*, and the like The Carving that was on the flat Part of the *Podium*, though not defcribed, we may eafily believe was of a Piece with the Painting, and perhaps only confifted of a Mixture of Leaves and Fruit, as are to be feen upon feveral ancient Pieces of Marble.

In

In Cornu Porticus ampliffimum Cubiculum, &c] The Rule which
Vitruvius lays down, *Lib.* 1 *Cap* 2 for the Symmetry to be obſerved in
proportioning Parts of a Building to the Whole, ſeems to have been obſerved by the Deſigner of theſe two *Villas* of *Pliny* For the *Cubiculum*
that was next the *Triclinium* in that ſmaller *Villa* of *Laurentinum,* and
was for the ſame End with this, was only ſtiled *Amplum,* but in this
Ampliffimum From the Windows of this Room which looked *Weſt-*
ward, there is no Mention of any other Proſpect but the *Xyſtus,* and
to make the *South* Proſpect of this vary from that of the *Triclinium,*
before the Windows was a Fountain, which *Pliny* commends as pleaſing
both the Eye and Ear Tho this Room was turned to the *South,* the
Breadth of the *Porticus* that was before it kept it ſhady in Summer,
when the Sun was oppoſite to it : Beſides theſe Conveniencies, this is
the only Room in this *Villa* where Proviſion was made for the Winter
by an *Hypocauſton,* which even in his other *Villa* is no where mentioned except in the Baths and Bed-Chambers; and 'tis not improbable that he made uſe of this for an *Hybernaculum,* which *Vitruvius*
directs to be turned to the Winter's ſetting Sun, as ſome of the
Windows of this Room were ; and the Sun, at its Winter Meridian
being low enough to caſt its Rays under the Roof of the *Porticus,*
warm'd it till almoſt Mid-day By ſome Paſſages we may collect that
he ſometimes paſſed the Beginning of the Winter at this Seat, for
which Reaſon he made ſuch Proviſion in this Room; and had, as will
afterwards appear, ſeveral other Rooms in this *Villa* proper to that
Seaſon, as he had as providently taken care for Summer Rooms in the
other *Villa*

Inde Apodyterium Balinei, &c] Tho' there were Rules for varying
the Diſpoſition of other Rooms according to the Seaſons in which they
were deſigned to be uſed, yet as has been obſerved in the Remarks
on *Laurentinum,* the Baths, whether they were built for Winter or
Summer Uſe, were always placed on the *Weſt* Side of the Houſe, ſo as
from thence to have a Proſpect of the ſetting Sun in the Winter's Sol-

E e   ſtice,

ftice, which Rule is followed in the placing thefe Baths   In thofe of
his leffer *Villa*, where he is more particular in his Defcription, there are
more Members defcribed than in this, tho' the *Apodyterium*, which
was the principal One, is mentioned only in this.   The Reafon for
this Room's being fo large, as he obferves, may probably be upon
Account of its Office, it being the Place where all thofe that bathed
undrefs'd, and returned to after their bathing, fweating, and Exercife
of the Ball ; and commodioufly to contain at once all thofe that
were before feperately employ'd in other Rooms   The Character of
hilare, which he gives to this Room, as well as to the *Cavadium* of
Laurentinum, feems to have been chofen, becaufe the Walls were
adorned with Ornaments of Architecture, Painting, or Sculpture ; and
not for its having been well lighted, which would have been a needlefs Commendation to a Court that had few Buildings about it higher
than one Story to fhade it.

Cella Frigidaria in qua, &c] This, as well as the *Apodyterium*, muft
certainly have been a very fpacious Room, containing a *Baptifterium*
large enough to fwim in, and a larger Bafon in its *Area*, round which
(according to the Directions of *Vitruvius*) muft have been a Place
feveral Feet wide to ftand on   The *Baptifterium*, which feems to
have been a Member common to all *Cella Frigidaria*, is here com-
mended upon the Account of its Darknefs ; a Quality perhaps efteemed
proper for a cold Bath, or as it rendred it more private, the *Pifcina*
being more publick, and for more than one to bathe in at a time

Frigidaria Cella connectitur Media, &c.] This which he calls the
middle Cell, was that of the middle Degree of Heat, betwixt the
Caldaria and *Frigidaria*, and was called the *Cella tepidaria.* Tho'
he mentions no other Heat than that of the Sun either in this or the
hot Cell, we may fuppofe, fince in the midft of Summer they could
not have Heat enough from his Body to caufe the Perfpiration required, they had other Affiftance from the *Hypocaufton*, that heated
the

Water; and the Sun is only mentioned to fhew, that when the
afon permitted, they drew all the Heat they could from it; pre-
ring that to the Heat of the Fire, from which they received as
tle Affiftance as they could.

Caldaria magis prominet enim, &c.] This *Cella* having Occafion
   more Heat than the other, is further advanced to the *Weft,* fo
it by its Projection it opportunely faced the Sun when nearer its
eridian, and confequently was more warm'd by it than the fore-
ntioned *Cella.* By the Defcription of this *Cella,* it feems as if
vided into three Parts, like three Rooms; two of which look-
   Southward, and faced the Sun before the Time of ufing them,
d barr'd the third, which lay to the *North,* from the Benefit of the
n at that time of the Day, by which Means that Divifion was
liged to make the greater Ufe of other Heat, and tho' farther
om the Sun, was perhaps as warm or warmer than the other
vo: And he obferves it did not fuffer the Inconveniency of be-
g dark, though removed farther from the Heat of the Sun To
efe Members of the Bath mentioned by our Author, in the Plan
e added others that were common to all Baths: the firft of which,
z the *Propnigeon* is placed fo as to communicate the Heat properly
   all the Sweating-Rooms, efpecially when they could receive no
ffiftance from the Sun, the *Hypocaufton,* that heated the Water
   well as the *Propnigeon,* is placed clofe to them; over which are
ree Veffels as *Vitruvius* directs, from whence the *Pifcina* that was
the *Area* of the *Cella Frigidaria* might not have been inconveni-
tly fupplied with Water On the other Side near the *Hypocaufton*
placed the *Unctuarium,* fo as (for Reafons before given) to have a
ommunication with the *Cella tepidaria* and *Apodyterium,* and to be
e neareft Part of the Baths to the *Sphærefterium.*

Apodyterio fuperpofitum eft Sphærefterium, &c] The Exercife that
as ufed in this Room requiring it to be very large, it was proper

to

to place it over the largeſt Member of the Baths, neither here nor in the *Villa* of *Laurentinum*, does he take Notice of any particular Qualities belonging to this Room, by which it appears that theſe Rooms were generally made after one common Method, and thoſe Circles for ſeveral kinds of Exerciſe that were uſed in this *Sphæreſterium* were probably no other than particular Marks that were made on the Floor; the Succeſs of their Play depending on the Ball's lighting in ſuch a Circle after it had been ſtruck, which was the Adverſaries Buſineſs to prevent; and the many ſorts of Exerciſe that this Room was made for, might be diverſified by Lines or Circles on the Walls or Floor, each Game having its particular Marks or Boundaries for the Ball, like the Game of Tennis, which tho' it takes up one entire Room, the ſame Place by making different Lines, may ſerve for ſeveral Games of the like Nature

Nec procul a Balineo, Scala, &c] Hitherto this Deſcription, like the greater Part of *Laurentinum*, has been on the Ground Floor, but now he aſcends, by Stairs which probably led to the *Sphæreſterium* as well as the *Cryptoporticus*, before he could reach to the latter there were three *Diæta*, which by his Account had nothing remarkable, except that each had a particular Proſpect The firſt ſeems to have been over the leſſer *Porticus*, and looked *Eaſtward*, having the *Sphæreſterium* on its Back, and its Windows had no other View but the Buildings that ſurrounded the Court, and the *Areola* it ſelf. The Second, which faced *Southward*, ſeems deſigned for a Winter Apartment by its warm Diſpoſition, and had the ſame Proſpect of the Meadows and Fields that the forementioned *Triclinium* had The Laſt, which lay in the direct Way from the Stairs to the *Cryptoporticus*, looked *Northward*, and was moſt properly diſpoſed for a Summer *Diæta* Beſides an agreeable Proſpect of the Vineyards that lay almoſt oppoſite to it, it had alſo the other Proſpects that the Hills afforded, but the Juttings of the Houſe hindered the View of the *Hippodrome*

In

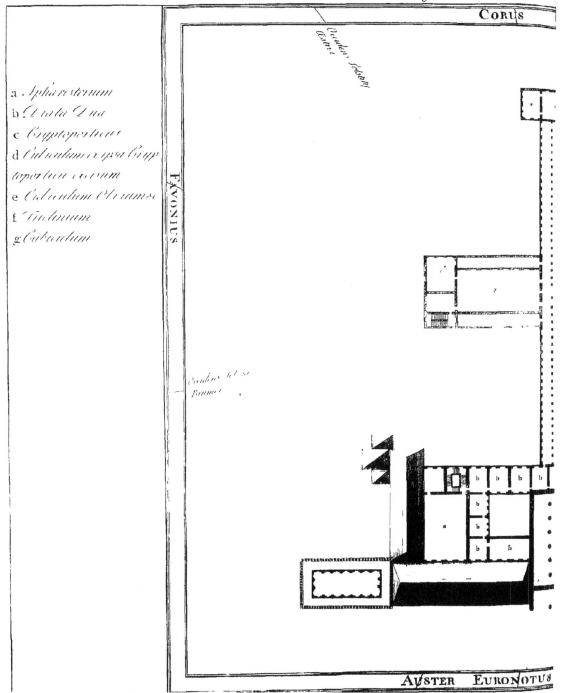

The PLAN of the seco

CORUS

a. Sphæristerium
b. Cubita Dua
c. Cryptoporticus
d. Cubiculum a ipsa Cryp-
toporticu cubitum
e. Cubiculum Obscurum
f. Triclinium
g. Cubiculum

FAVONIUS

AUSTER   EURONOTUS

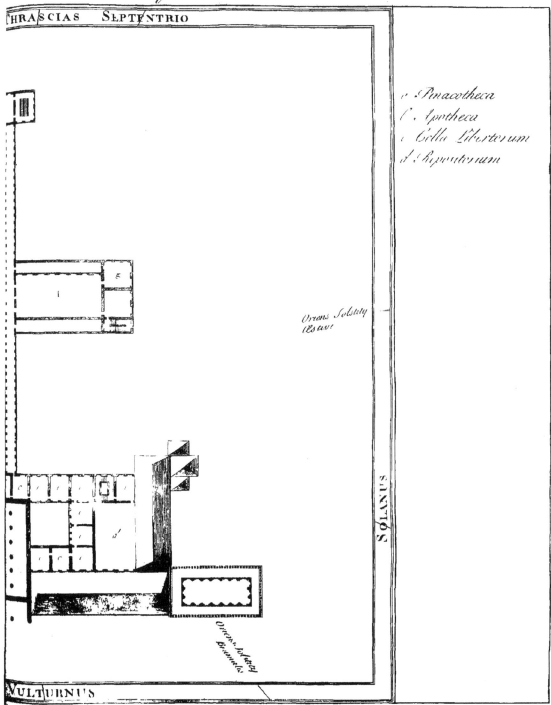

THRASCIAS   SEPTENTRIO

a *Pinacotheca*
b *Apotheca*
c *Cella Libertorum*
d *Repositorium*

Oriens Solstity Æstiva

SOLANUS

Oriens Æquin. Brumale

VULTURNUS

In summa Cryptoporticus Cubiculum, &c] From these *Diætæ,* before
he proceeds in his Description, he passes through the *Cryptoporticus;*
at the Head or most *Northern* Part of which was a *Cubiculum,* probably as wide as the *Cryptoporticus* itself, being said to be cut off
from it: The Disposition of it shews it wholly to be designed for a
Summer Room, those Prospects from it that are mentioned lying
North of the *Villa*

Jungitur Cubiculum obvium, &c.] The Office of the foregoing
Room seems likely to have been a Place of Retirement when fatigu'd
with walking in the *Cryptoporticus,* and that there might not be a
Room wanting for the same Use in a colder Season, this Room was
provided, whose Windows looking contrary to the other, and by its
jutting out causing an Angle, must have been warmed, during most
of the Winter after Mid-day

Hinc oritur Diæta, &c] This *Diæta* that joyns the *Villa* to the *Hippodrome* can't be said to do so, if upon the same Floor with the *Cryptoporticus,* therefore we may reasonably conclude, though being not
mentioned, he here descends in his Description   By its Disposition it
must have been very pleasant in Summer, and being joyn'd to the
Hippodrome must have had a thorough Prospect of it, which he has
not thought fit to take much Notice of, because he is afterwards
very particular in the Description of that Piece of Art; and it may be
observed that *Pliny* is no where so particular in mentioning artificial as
natural Prospects · And where both are seen, he neglects to take Notice of the former, as perhaps not thinking them so beautiful as the
other   The Stairs, which in the Plan lead to the *Diæta,* answer the
Cubiculum last mentioned.

Hæc Facies hic Visus a Fronte, &c] This Front was that part of
the House that lay most *Northward,* and which he has just described,
and was the Garden Front of the House, or rather the Front of that

Part of it that lay neareft to the Garden   This *Cryptoporticus* is here
ftyled *æftiva*, becaufe it was placed in that part of the *Villa* that was
moft agreeable in Summer, and beft defended from the Sun, as was
that which lay from the *South* to the *North*, and the Windows
opened to the *Eaft* and *Weft*, as thefe of the *Cryptoporticus* did; fo
that the Sun in its Meridian only fhone on its Roof, and when lower,
was in a great Meafure kept off by the moft *Southern* Parts of the
Houfe, and was altogether cool at the Time it was wanted, which
was rather before than after Mid-day

In Edito pofita, &c] As the laft Rooms were below Stairs, *Pliny*
would now have us underftand that this Room he is about to
fpeak of was upon the Floor from which he had juft defcended to
take Notice of that *Diæta*, and the lofty Situation of this *Cryptoporticus* was the Reafon he took fuch particular Notice of the Profpect of
the Vineyards from it, which could be feen over whatever obftructed
that View in the Rooms that lay lower than this, which had only a
Profpect of what grew on the Hills above the Vines; but this com-
manded the lower Parts of thofe Hills, and had fuch a full View of
them, that to thofe that walked in it, they feemed to have been
very near

In media Triclinium, &c] In the Difpofition of the former *Triclinium*, there was fo much Regard had to the Profpects, that tho' all
the Means that Art could invent were made ufe of to prevent its being
at particular Times rather too hot, it could no ways be avoided; but
that he might not appear lefs provident in this than in his Winter
Villa, had fo difpofed this other Room for Entertainments, that it was
fhelter'd to the *South* by the greater Part of the Houfe, on which
Side it appears to have had no Windows, and was quite hid from
the *Weftern* Sun by the Interpofition of the *Cryptoporticus*, and on the
North lay the *Apennines*, from the Vallies of which it was cool'd by
refrefhing Breezes, which was more particularly taken Notice of here,
becaufe

...ufe it was a moie than ordinary Advantage to a Room that was
...fe in Summer, before the Heat of the Day was much abated · Be-
on the fame Floor with the *Cryptoporticus,* its Profpe8s are the
e with That, for the Vineyaids were not confined to one Side of
Houfe, but by *Pliny*'s own Account, were one continued Traft at
Bottom of the Hills; fo that from the Windows that lookt one
y, and from the Folding-doors that opened almoft oppofite the
ndows of the *Cryptoporticus,* were prefented two Views of thefe
...eyards

A Latere Triclinii, &c] As thofe, that were come to the *Triclinium*
...the Stairs that weie near the Baths, were obliged to pafs through
...ral Rooms in their Way to it, it was requifite to have others at
...fame time without this Inconveniency; and thefe were for that
...fon placed on the *South* Side of the *Triclinium,* which was neareft
Entrance of the Houfe

In Fine Cubiculum, &c] Accoiding to Cuftom, near this *Triclinium*
a *Cubiculum*; the Difpofition of which feems to have made it as
per for Summer as the *Triclinium* itfelf, and its Piofpeds are the
e, for tho' the *Cryptoporticus* is only mentioned to be feen from
Room, it muft alfo have been fo fiom the othei, though but
quely.

ubeft Cryptoporticus Subterranea, &c] This *Cryptoporticus,* that
under the *Triclinium,* feems in all Refpe8s to have been like
at prefent is called a Giotto, and in *Italy* is efteemed a neceffary
t for the Pleafuic of a Summer *Villa* This Place thus guarded
m the Sun, might be thought fufficiently cool, without any Affi-
ce from thofe Airs that refiefhed the *Triclinium,* yet we may ima-
e that (tho' not mentioned) the Light was admitted into it, other-
e the Room, tho' cool, muft have been unpleafant

Poſt utramque Cryptoporticum, &c.] *Vitruvius*'s directions to
Houſes for hot Climates more open than for cold, have been care
obſerved by the Deſigner of this *Villa*, there being no leſs than
Porticus proper for walking in, mentioned in this *Villa*, and in *Lar
tinum* there was but one, and that well guarded from the V
and the Weather   This laſt *Porticus* ſeems to have been of ſing
Uſe, for ſtanding from *South* to *North* as the *Cryptoporticus*
which it ſupported, it gave a thorough Paſſage to all Airs that
from the cooleſt Quarters, and conſequently muſt cauſe great Refr
ment to the Rooms that lay below, eſpecially thoſe that lay *Weſt* o
which otherwiſe by confining the Rays of the Sun, muſt, towards
Declenſion of the Day in Summer, have been much warmer
Character which he gives this *Porticus* of being *Hyberna ante*, &c
have been ſpoken, with relation to its being warm or cold at thoſe T
of the Day, it being cool by its Airs, and being well guarded fron
Sun during the Time of Exerciſe, which was commonly before
day, ſo that its being warm after that Hour was no great Inconveni
to it.

Hac adeuntur Diæta dua, &c] By the Deſcription of theſe App
ments we may reaſonably infer that One was deſigned for Sum
and the Other for Winter, as having before obſerved He no w
in this *Villa* takes Notice of any Benefit of the Sun, but in Ro
proper for the colder Seaſon, or in thoſe that required extrac
nary Heat, as the Sweating Rooms   The low Diſpoſition of t
Diæta, and their Views being intercepted by the other Parts of
Houſe, is probably the Reaſon why he makes no Mention of
Proſpect from them

Hanc Diſpoſitionem Amœnitatemque Tectorum, &c.] As this Deſc
tion began with the Avenue, or thoſe Parts that lay on the Fron
the Houſe, ſo it cloſed with the Garden that lay *North*, or on
Back of it, which conſiſted of two principal Parts, *viz*   that w

is here called the *Hippodrome*, and that which lay beyond it This first Part feems to have had its Name from its refembling thofe publick Places fo called (the Difference betwixt which and the *Circus* has been fhewn in the Notes on this Epiftle) rather than from their Exercife of Horfe-racing; for which the *Geftatio* might as well have ferved as for that of the Coach, unlefs perhaps this may have been fometimes ufed upon the Account of Shade, which the other had not, nor did much want, fince the *Vehicula* were covered at Top, and their Sides enclofed by Curtains The *Circus* and *Hippodrome* had this in common, that they had both the Middle of their *Areas* filled up with fmall Buildings, Arches, Obelisks, Altars, or the like, but this lying next the Houfe, and its Beauties confifting in the Ornaments of the Boundaries, it was thought proper to omit thofe Reprefentations of Buildings that he had in the *Geftatio*, which here would have intercepted the Profpect from thofe Rooms that lay next the *Hippodrome*, which feems to be what he means by *Medius patefiat* The Planes that were the principal Trees with which this Place was bounded, were in moft of the Gardens of the antient *Romans*, and were valued upon the Account of their extraordinary Shade That thefe might not only pleafe by their Shade and Leaves, their Bodies were made Supporters to Ivy, that was planted about them, which covered not only the Trunks, but alfo the Boughs, and as he obferves, join'd the Trees as it were into one Body; by which Means the Shade muft have been increafed, and the Sun kept off as much as by the Roof of a *Porticus*, to whofe Pillars their Trunks bore a Refemblance: Befides, as the principal Rooms look'd towards this Place, and as it has been obferved he fometimes ftaid at this *Villa* a fmall Part of the Winter, at that Seafon the Leaves from the Planes were the lefs miffed, fince the Laurel, Box, and Cyprefs-Trees (that helped to fence and fhade this *Hippodrome*) at all Seafons afforded an agreeable Profpect, which was increafed by the different Degrees of Colour that were between thefe forementioned Ever-greens

Rectus

Rectus hic Hippodromi Limes, &c] Before any Notice be taken of
that Part that lay beyond the *Hippodrome*, which is the only *Roman*
Garden whofe Defcription is come down to us, it may not be improper to enquire into the firft Rife of Gardens, and of what they at
firft confifted, by which a Judgment may be the better paffed on this
before us   The Invention of this Art feems to have been owing to
the firft Builders of *Villas*, who were naturally led to fearch for the
moft beautiful Places in which to build them, but as it was hardly
poffible to meet with any, that within the Compafs defigned for the
Pleafure of the *Villa*, fhould contain every thing that was compleatly
agreeable, it was neceffary to fupply by Care and Induftry whatever
was wanting in the natural Face of the Country: but at firft they
aimed at nothing further than the Difpofition of their Plantations, for
by the fmall Knowledge we can arrive at, in the Gardens of the firft
Ages, they feem to have been no more than felect, well-water'd Spots
of Ground, irregularly producing all forts of Plants and Trees, grateful either to the Sight, Smell, or Tafte, and refrefhed by Shade and
Water · Their whole Art confifting in little more than in making
thofe Parts next their *Villas* as it were accidentally produce the choiceft
Trees, the Growth of various Soils, the Face of the Ground fuffering
little or no Alteration, the Intent of Gardens being within a fixt Compafs of Ground, to enjoy all that Fancy could invent moft agreeable
to the Senfes   But this rough Manner, not appearing fufficiently beautiful to thofe of a more regular and exact Tafte, fet them upon in-
venting a Manner of laying out the Ground and Plantations of Gardens by the Rule and Line, and to trim them up by an Art that was
vifible in every Part of the Defign   By the Accounts we have of the
prefent Manner of Defigning in *China*, it feems as if from the two
former Manners a Third had been formed, whofe Beauty confifted in
a clofe Imitation of Nature; where, tho' the Parts are difpofed with
the greateft Art, the Irregularity is ftill preferved; fo that their Manner may not improperly be faid to be an artful Confufion, where there
is no Appearance of that Skill which is made ufe of, their *Rocks,*

Cafcades,

Cafcades, and *Trees,* bearing their natural Forms In the Difpofition of *Pliny's* Garden, the Defigner of it fhews that he was not unacquainted with thefe feveral Manners, and the Whole feems to have been a Mixture of them all Three In the *Pratulum* Nature appears in her plaineft and moft fimple Drefs; fuch as the firft Builders were contented with about their *Villas,* when the Face of the Ground it felf happened to be naturally beautiful. By the Care ufed in regulating the turning and winding Walks, and cutting the Trees and Hedges into various Forms, is fhewn the Manner of the more regular Gardens, and in the *Imitatio Ruris,* he feems to hint at the third Manner, where, under the Form of a beautiful Country, *Hills, Rocks, Cafcades, Rivulets, Woods, Buildings,* &c were poffibly thrown into fuch an agreeable Diforder, as to have pleafed the Eye from feveral Views, like fo many beautiful Landskips; and at the fame time have afforded at leaft all the Pleafures that could be enjoy'd in the moft regular Gardens The main Body of this Garden was difpofed after the Second of thefe three Manners; through its winding Paths One as it were accidentally fell upon thofe Pieces of a rougher Tafte, that feem to have been made with a Defign to furprize thofe that arrived at them, through fuch a Scene of Regularities, which (in the Opinion of fome) might appear more beautiful by being near thofe plain Imitations of Nature, as Lights in Painting are heightened by Shades The Intent of this Garden (befides pleafing the Eye, being to afford Shade and Coolnefs in the hotter Seafon of the Year) required it to be well ftockt with Trees and Water; which laft we may fuppofe took its feeming natural Courfe through the rougher Parts of the Garden, and in the regular appeared in a more artful Difpofition; as did alfo the Trees, which both here and in thofe Parts on the *South* Side, or Front of the *Villa,* were cut into unwarrantable Forms, if the Ornaments of Gardens are allow'd to be only Imitations of Nature's Productions; for it cannot be fuppofed that Nature ever did or will produce Trees in the Form of Beafts, or Letters, or any Refemblance of Embroidery, which Imitations rather belong to the Statuary, and

Workers

Workers with the Needle than the Architect, and tho' pleasing in those Arts, appear monstrous in this. Tho' it is plain that this Manner of adorning Gardens was not at that Time a new Invention, since as has been observed in the former Part of this Work, *Varro* in his Description of his *Ornithon*, mentions the *Parterre* that lay near it: And this Custom was got to such a Head in the Time of *Pliny*, that the Gardeners, from clipping and laying out every thing by the Line, and turning Trees and Hedges into various Forms, were called *Topiarii*; and it is easy to think that in Compliance to the Fashion, the Architect of this *Villa*, tho' we see he knew better, was induced to make use of those Ornaments As to the several Names, which were formed by the Box-Hedges of this Garden, we cannot be certain of any but One, which was that of the Master The Liberty that is taken of naming *Mustius* in the Plan as his Architect, is because it appears by the 36th *Ep* of the Ninth Book of *Pliny*, that he did some Work for him near this *Villa*

Post has Acanthus, &c] Betwixt this Garden and the Garden Buildings lay a Walk, made soft to the Feet (as the Custom then was) with the *Acanthus*, which therefore gives Name to a Part that he could not have properly called a *Xystus* or *Ambulatio*; as, for a Reason of the same Nature, the Walk in *Laurentinum* is called *Vinea*, from its being covered with Vines

In Capite Stibadium, &c] The *South* Side of this Garden was bounded by Cypress-Trees for the Sake of their Shade, and on the *North* stood a fixed Bed of Marble, from whence as they lay at their Meals, they could perhaps command the Prospect of the greater Part of the Garden· To keep the Heat of the Sun from this Place, there was a sort of open Roof to it, covered only with Vine Branches and Leaves, and supported by four Marble Pillars, so that no Air was kept out, nor any Prospect interrupted Under this Covert all necessary Care seems to have been taken for eating in a very cool Manner

ner, for from the Bed they lay on the Water flow'd out; inftead
of a Table, their Food fwam about in a Bafon, which was filled
by the Water that came from the *Stibadium*; and that it was
their Cuftom to lye higher, or at leaft as high as their Tables
may be feen, by the following Draught of an *antique Bafs Re-
leive*, which that noble Encourager of Arts the Earl of *Pembroke*
preferves in his ineftimable Collection of Antiquities at *Wilton*.

The Drynefs of the Manner of Defigning, inftead of making it lefs
valuable, ferves to prove its Antiquity, which may be confirmed by
the Figure of *Hebe*, who was feigned to be difcarded from waiting
on *Jupiter* about the Time of the *Trojan* War This Piece, which is
about three Feet in Length, and two Feet in Height, is at prefent as
entire as in the Drawing, where may be feen that nothing is wanting
but the right Arm of *Minerva*, which probably was raifed higher
than the reft of the Work, and held her Spear, as the other Hand
did her Shield The Reafon *Pliny* takes Notice of this Bafon's being

continually full, was to shew its Use, which being that of a Table, it was requisite its Superficies should be always at a fixt Height, which was easily brought about by those Conveyances, that carried off the Water which lay lower than the Margin, to prevent the Water's flowing over What the *Gustatorium & Cœnatio* were, have been explain'd in the Notes on this Epistle, where they are shewn to have been the Vessels on which they served up their Victuals at different Meals; and that it was customary before *Pliny*'s Time to have several Fancies and Devices on their Table Furniture, appears from *Petronius*'s Description of the *Cœnatio* of *Trimalcio*, that had the twelve Signs of the *Zodiack* separately designed in one Circle, each serving for a different Dish: tho' it is indeed mentioned, and at the same time ridiculed by him as a fantastick Invention, yet the Devices on those of *Pliny* seem to be properly enough adapted to the Table, the Figures of Water-Fowls and Boats being Fancies natural enough for such a Bason.

Contra Fons egerit Aquam, &c] This Fountain that lay before the *Stibadium* seems to have been thus disposed to increase the Pleasure of the Prospect, and add to the Coolness of the Place The Advantage of a falling Water, which was not wanting about this *Villa*, set the Designer upon contriving several Water-works; Five of which *Pliny* has given some slight Account of, the First was that in the *Areola*, resembling an overflowing Bowl the next was in a *Cubiculum*, that lookt into the same *Areola*, which also had its Water falling from a Bowl, tho' not in the same Manner as the other · for as the one ran over at the Top, the other by its Description seems to have had its Water issuing through Pipes like Holes in the Sides of the Bowl The Third was that before the Window of the first-mentioned *Cubiculum*, and was designed in Imitation of a *Cascade*, the Water only falling from on High The Fourth, was the *Stibadium*, from whence the Water flowing out had an agreeable Effect, and expressed a Motion very proper to it, which whenever pressed down by any Weight, makes its Passage through the first Opening it finds. By what has been before observed ferved about Gardens, it does not appear there are more than two forts, *viz.* the Natural, or thofe that are feemingly fo, and the Artificial or Regular · fo neither do we find there can be more than two Manners for defigning Fountains, *viz* that wherein Nature is clofely imitated, as in the *Cafcades* from Rocks or Hills, or elfe that more artificial Manner, where tho' all the Ornaments are the vifible Works of Art, yet ftill the Water feems to receive its Motion from a natural Caufe, as in thofe Fountains juft now taken Notice of; and tho' each fort may without Error be ufed in either Manner of Gardens, yet certainly they are moft properly introduced in thofe whofe Manner they imitate. This feems to have been the Opinion of the Architect who defigned the Fountains about this *Villa,* for here the Gardens being for the moft Part extreamly regular, he could not think proper to introduce any rougher Manner in his Water-works, tho' he does not feem to have had fo much Regard to Juftnefs in the Defigns themfelves; fince if he had, he muft have omitted or altered this that ftood before the *Stibadium* (which was the fifth Fountain propofed to be taken Notice of) for fhould it be allowed that Fountains, like other Works of Art, ought to be formed by this Rule, that they fhould imitate the Truth, or at leaft the *Verifimilitude,* in this Defign he has certainly erred, fince it has little or no Refemblance to any probable Motion of Water, which is feldom feen from a natural Caufe to rife perpendicularly to any Degree of Height What can be beft faid in the Defence of this Water-work is, that it is of a Piece with the other forced Fancies in the ornamental Parts of this Garden

E Regione Stibadii, &c] In thefe Garden-Buildings there was no Provifion made for the Night, as in that of *Laurentinum* ; there being lefs Occafion for it here, where the Houfe it felf was placed (as it were) in the Middle of a Garden : fo that this feems only to have been defigned for the Enjoyment of fome few Hours in greater Retirement At a fmall Diftance from the *Stibadium* there were two Rooms, One of which anfwers the Defcription of our Summer-Houfes, and the

Other

Other was only a fmall One contiguous to it   This Building was covered all over with Greens, except the Part next the *Stibadium*, and
that was cafed with Marble , which it is obfervable *Pliny* now here omits
to mention through his whole Defcription, whenever the leaft Piece is
made ufe of from whence it may be concluded, that the Walls of
his Buildings were made of coarfer Stuff, as he very well knew that the
Elegance of a Defign did not confift in the Richnefs of the Materials
Befides the Covering of the *Cubiculum*, there is nothing material taken
Notice of but the two Ranges of Windows ; whofe Number was
perhaps increafed for the fame Reafon with thofe in the *Cryptoporticus*,
that when the Sun grew troublefome, the lower Range might have
been fhut, and the other opened, to admit the Air and Light that
was necffary

Mox Zothecula, &c] This Room muft have been parted from the
Cubiculum, as the *Zotheca* of the other *Villa* was from the *Heliocaminus*, by Glafs Doors and Curtains ; which when opened, this little
Room became as it were part of the *Cubiculum*, and when fhut, was
a Room by it felf The other *Zotheca* was large enough to contain
a Bed and two Chairs, but This a Bed only ; and by the Account he
gives of it, muft have been defigned for the fame Ufe with the other,
fince it in all Things refembled it, except the feveral diftant Profpects, this having no other than that of the neighbouring Greens ·
but by the Fountain that was in it, we fee Regard was had for Refrefhment during the Summer   The Profpect which *Pliny* hints to
have been kept from the *Stibadium* by the Interpofition of thefe two
Rooms, was perhaps nothing elfe, but the Greens that lay beyond
it, or it may be thofe Hills and Woods that lay *North* of the *Villa*.
The following Drawing may ferve to illuftrate the Difpofition and
Form of the *Stibadium* and Buildings laft defcribed.

Sunt Locis pluribus difposita Sedilia, &c.] The Seats that were in several Parts of this Garden, as well as the *Stibadium,* were of Marble ; not only because they were exposed to the Weather, but for Coolness Sake, to which the small Fountains that were near them did not a little contribute, and at the same time add to the Beauty of the Place   The Plenty of Water, that is mentioned to have been upon such a rising Ground, was very likely brought by Art to one general *Refervoir,* from whence the Pleasures of the Gardens, and Conveniencies of the House were sufficiently supplied, its first Appearance seems to have been at the Head of the Garden, which if we suppose the highest Ground, from thence it might have easily supplied all the other Fountains and Neceffaries both of House and Gardens · and as he obferves in its Paffage have watered the Greens of the Gardens and *Hippodrome*

Nifi propofuiffem omnes Angulos tecum Epiftola circumire, &c] By these Words, and what is said some few Lines after, one might think *Pliny* had given a compleat Defcription of every Part in and about this *Villa* ; but upon Examination it will be found that he only defcribed what was for the Use and Pleafure of Himself and Friends : For in this *Villa* he has not mentioned any Rooms peculiar to the Servants, as he has in that of *Laurentinum,* and has omitted the mentioning any thing that lay on the *Eaft* Side of the *Atrium,* where very probably he had Offices neceffary to the *Villa Urbana,* and Lodgings for the proper Servants, as the *Atrienfes, Topiarii, Comœdi,* &c Befides which Rooms of inferiour Ufe, those which were common to the Houses of Great Men (as the *Bafilica, Bibliotheca,* and *Pinacotheca*) are placed in the Plan according to the Directions of *Vitruvius*

Amo enim quæ maxima ex Parte ipfe inchoavi aut inchoata percolui, &c] If in the Defcription of his Garden he had not mentioned the Artificer feparate from the Mafter of the *Villa,* this Paffage might give some Caufe to imagine that *Pliny* was himself the Architect

I 1

Habes

Habes caufas cur ego Thufcos meos Tufculanis, Tyburtinis, Praneftinifque meis praponam, &c.] *Pliny* in his Epiftles has mentioned no lefs than feven of his *Villas*, and gives us to underftand that he had feveral more, and not only the Situations of thofe two he has defcribed, but thofe of the three other *Villas* here mentioned are efteemed at prefent the fineft of that Conntry; yet not content with all thefe, he had alfo feveral on the Lake near his native *Comum* The Situations of two of which, as defcribed by him *Lib* 9 *Ep* 7 gave Occafion to take Notice of them in the Remarks on *Laurentinum* Thofe *Villas* of *Tufculum*, *Tibur* and *Pranefte* being fo near *Rome*, and in Places of fuch Note, and to which fo many reforted from the City, when he was there, he was obliged to wear the Habit proper to his Quality, and was not much lefs incommoded with Bufinefs than at *Rome* which (by means of the Diftance that *Tufcum* lay from the City) he was intirely free from, except what happened by his Neighbourhood to the Town of *Tifernum*, of which, *Lib* 4 *Ep* 1 he tells us he was, while very young, chofen *Patron* To this Quiet which he enjoyed here, he attributes an additional Health to the Place The Method of fpending his Time here, befides thofe Hours which were taken up in the neceffary Offices of Life, he wholly employ'd in exercifing his Mind by Study, and his Body by Hunting, both which Inclinations (as appears, *Lib.* 9 *Ep* 3) he gratified at one and the fame Time; fince he never followed the latter Diverfion without providing for the former, and always carried his Writing Tables with him As his Application to Study appears in many Places of his Epiftles, fo his Fondnefs for Hunting has caufed him to be rallied by *Corn Tacitus*, to whom he therefore wrote his fixth Epiftle of the firft Book, in Defence of this Method of fpending his Time

This *Tufcan Villa*, not lefs than that of *Laurentinum*, would deferve the Cenfure of *Varro*, had we not (for what has been before obferved concerning the large Eftate he had here) Reafon to believe there was a Farm-Houfe not far removed from the other,

and

and all other Neceffaries of Life; upon this Authority, in the following Plan I have prefumed to add thofe Things omitted by *Pliny*, conformable to preceeding Rules, and which I fhall endeavour to explain. On each Side of the Pleafure-Garden is the *Vivarium*; one Part of which is allotted to the Ufe of thofe Beafts that *Varro* fays were confined in fuch Enclofures near their *Villas*, as *Hares, Deers, wild Boars*, &c the other is for thofe Fowls that were kept in great Numbers near, tho' not within the Walls of the *Villa*, as *Geefe, Ducks, Peacocks*, &c. and in both are Ponds for *Fifh* The Plans of fmall Buildings that are in feveral Parts of the *Vivarium* (except thofe for the Ufe of the forementioned Fowls) are fome defigned as Pleafure-Houfes, and others for the Ufe of the Keeper, and fuch Servants as were neceffary within the *Vivarium*, viz *Hunters, Fowlers* and *Fifhermen*. On the right Hand of the Avenue, that leads to the *Villa Urbana*, on the Brow of the fame Hill, and fronting the fame Way, is the *Villa Ruftica*, containing Conveniencies for *Man, Beaft, Fowl*, &c. that were within the Walls of the *Villa* itfelf, tho' fomething different from thofe Manners in the former Part of the Work. Oppofite to the Entrance of the Farm-Houfe, and betwixt the Road and River is the Temple of *Ceres*, mentioned by *Pliny*, *Lib.* 9 *Ep.* 39. and by the fame Meadow wherein the Temple ftood is an Ofier Ground, which was near all their *Villas*. On the Back of the *Villa Ruftica* is the Fruit Garden or *Pomarium*, and betwixt the Farm Yard and the Avenue of the *Villa Urbana*, is the Kitchen Garden; oppofite to which, on the other Side of the Avenue (in a Grove planted and cut regularly) is the *Apiary*, that was commonly furrounded by flowery Shrubs, and with fmall Streams of Water near it, and oppofite to the *Apiary*, is the *Cochleare* furrounded by Water. On the other Side of the *Apiary* is the *Glirarium*, fill'd with Trees that bear Maft or Acorns, as *Varro* directs On that Part of the Plan which is obferv'd by *Pliny* to be on higher Ground than where the Houfe ftood, is an *Aquaduct*; which may be prefum'd fupplied his *Garden* and *Villa* as he mentions, and which after having paffed the *Vivarium*, and furnifhed all the Offices

of

of both *Villas,* enters the *Tiber* by a Mill that is placed near the Temple of *Ceres.* The rest of this Plan, that contains Meadows, Vineyards, Woods, plowed Land, *&c.* will be found on Examination to answer *Pliny's* Description: but the whole may be better understood by the following *Index.*

A   Tuscum, *the* Villa *of* Pliny

a.   *The* Gestatio, *or Place for the Exercise of the Chariot*

b   *The* Ambulatio, *or Walk surrounding the Terraces*

c   *The Slope, with the Forms of Beasts cut in Box*

d   *The* Xystus *or Terrace before the* Porticus, *and on the Sides of the House*

e   *The* Hippodrome, *or Plain so called, on the North Side of the House.*

f   *Plane Trees on the straight Bounds of the* Hippodrome

g   *Cypress Trees on the Semicircular Bounds of the* Hippodrome

h   *The* Stibadium, *and other Buildings in the Garden.*

i   *Box cut into Names and other Forms*

k.   *The* Pratulum *or little Meadow in the Garden*

l   *The Imitation of the natural Face of some Country, in the Garden*

m   *The Walk covered with* Acanthus *or Moss*

n   *The Meadows that lay before the* Gestatio

o   *The Tops of the Hills covered with aged Trees*

p   *The Underwood on the Decline of the Hills*

q   *Vineyards below the Underwoods*

r   *Cornfields*

s   *The River* Tyber.

t   *The Temple of* Ceres *built by* Mustius

B.   *The Farm House*

C.   *The* Vivarium *or Park.*

D.   *The Kitchen Garden*

E.   *The Orchard.*

F.   *The* Apiary.

G   *A Place for Snails call'd* Cochleare

H   *The* Glirarium *or Place to keep Dormice in*

I   *An Osier Ground.*

K.   *The* Aquæduct.

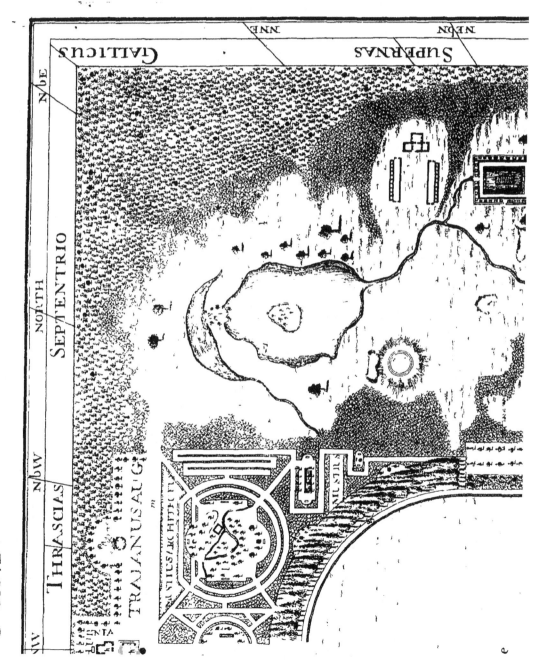

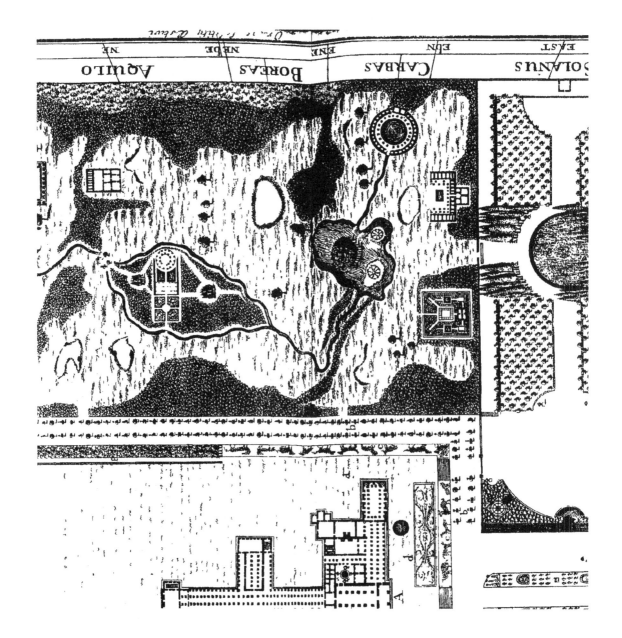

EAST · SOLANUS · ESE · CARBAS · ENE · BOREAS · NEDE · NE · AQUILO

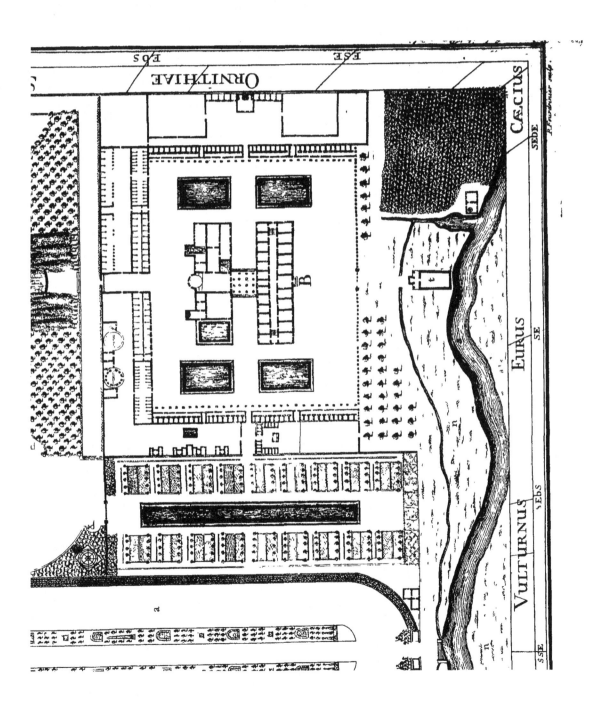

ORNITHIAE

EOS

ESE

CÆCIUS

SEDE

B

EURUS

SE

VULTURNUS

SEbS

SSE

P. Fourdrinier sculp.

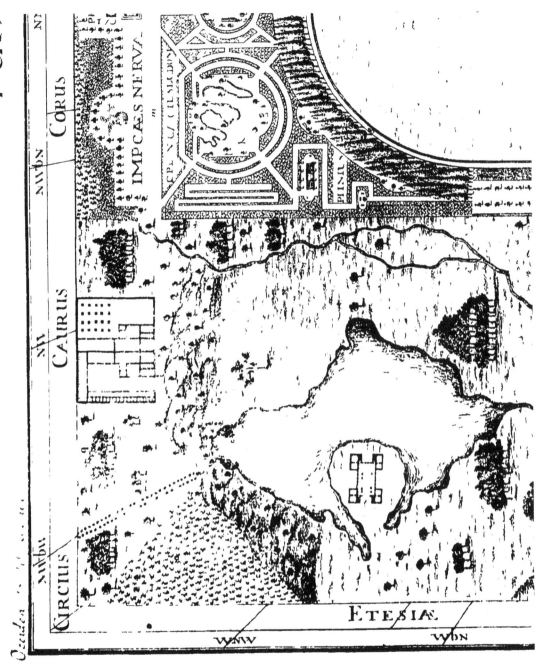

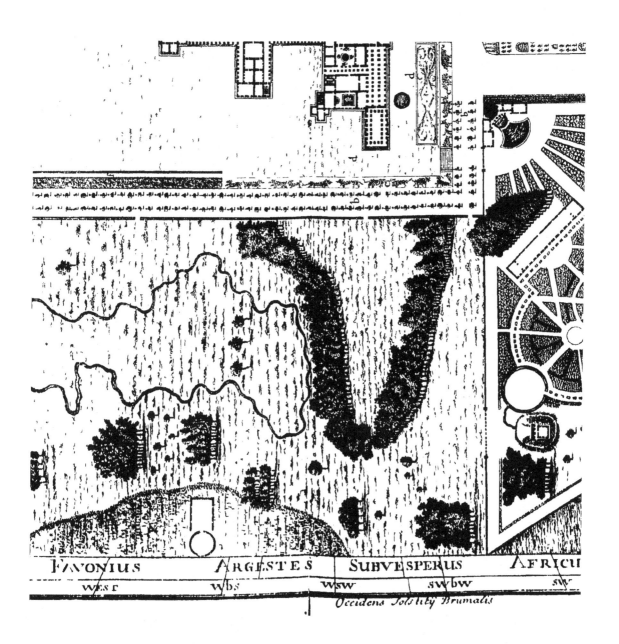

FAVONIUS   ARGESTES   SUBVESPERUS   AFRICU

west   wbs   wsw   swbw   sw

Occidens Solstity Brumalis

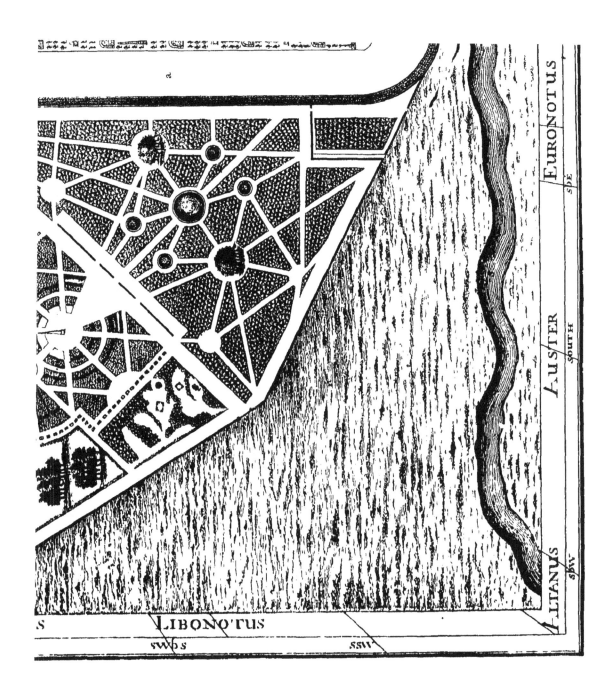

EURONOTUS

S DE

AUSTER

SOUTH

ALTANUS

S W

LIBONOTUS

S W b S

S S W

S

IF in the foregoing *Work* the *Art of building* Villas *has been reduced to some Method, my Labours have not been entirely thrown away, since all Writings that contain Rules for any Art whatever, become more or less valuable according as those Rules are well or ill digested into order.*

The Villa of Laurentinum *shews what the Architect ought to observe, that would build a pleasant and convenient House on such a Situation, for a Person of* Pliny's *Taste and Quality. In the second Part I have endeavour'd to set forth the several Particulars which were observ'd by the Ancients in the Choice of Situations, and by several Examples to shew the Disposition of every Part about the* Villa, *but more especially those belonging to the* Farm house *and Places built for Profit and the Conveniences of Cattle, Fowls, &c. In the third Part has been seen the same Architect which probably built* Laurentinum, *judiciously varying the Rules he observed in that* Villa, *and adapting them to an House built upon a very different Situation, and for a different Season of the Year, as if he had endeavoured in the Disposition of these two, to shew the Rules necessary to be observed in building all Country Houses of Pleasure. And tho' the Difference of Customs and Climates makes some of them seem of little Use in a more Northern Country, yet to the judicious Architect there are few Parts of either* Villa *of* Pliny, *that may not one Time or another be of Service even here, particularly of* Laurentinum, *That, as has been observed, being built for a* Winter Villa, *the Risings and Settings of the Sun indeed are mark'd in the Plans as proper to the Latitude of those Parts of* Italy *near* Rome.

Pliny, *whose* Villas *are the principal Subject of this Work, was (as may appear by his Writings) a Person of excellent Judgment in all the polite Arts, and as he lived under* Trajan *had an Opportunity of seeing the Performances of, and advising with* Apollodorus, *one of the greatest Architects that any Age produced, but whether this Artist, or* Mustius *that was sometimes employed by* Pliny, *or* Pliny *himself de-*

K k   *sign'd*

sign'd thefe Villas, *is not to be determin'd, but this is certain, that the Defcriptions of them by* Pliny *fhew that He was perfectly acquainted with the whole that was neceffary to be underftood in their Situation and Difpofition.*

INDEX.

INDEX

Lightning Source UK Ltd.
Milton Keynes UK
UKOW04f2241081116
287199UK00014B/937/P